Everything You've Been Taught About Sales Is Wrong* (*Probably)

How to Make More Sales in a Way That Feels Really Good For You (and Your Clients)

Anna Payne

authors
AND CO.

Contents

Dedication

This book is for all of you who dream of making life better through entrepreneurship and have the courage to go out and make it happen.

It is for the dreamers, the doers, the misfits, those who are called unrealistic, who worry they are too much or too ambitious, those who quietly wonder if they are enough. (You are!)

It is for those who never quite feel they belong in the traditional places and are turned off by traditional ways of creating sales and success.

Let's create success on your terms and build a good business that does good things in the world!

The average human has four thousand weeks to live. Don't waste any of those precious weeks waiting and worrying. If you take only one thing from the book, let it be this: Have the courage to start before you feel ready.

Note From the Author

You can be the best in the world at what you do, but that doesn't matter if you can't make sales consistently. The harsh reality is that your business will fail. Others who are not as good as you but are better at selling will succeed.

Being good at what you do and having a website or popping the odd post about it on social media is not enough to build a successful business. The answer is a sales strategy that delivers a consistent, repeatable (and ideally scalable) flow of sales.

If you are a business owner and you need to create or improve your sales strategy, you are in the right place! This book will help you understand the key components of a successful sales strategy with a stack of practical examples, tools and checklists at each stage, so you can create a plan that delivers sales on repeat and build a successful business, doing what you love.

I will also show you that at every step of the way, selling is really about serving and building long-term relationships, showing up as a person of value and making people's lives better somehow... happier, healthier or wealthier.

Contrary to popular belief, good selling isn't about pushing, forcing, persuading or any other negative words.

But it's easy to understand why you might think that. You've probably heard of some of the standard practices in sales. You've almost definitely experienced them as a consumer:

- **Spray and pray:** Pitch to as many people as possible with no real strategy but hoping due to volume that something will stick.
- **Price withholding:** Don't disclose the price until the very end of a conversation, after you've 'closed' the customer on the value of the product or service. (And then you must stay silent, waiting for the prospective client to speak after you've said the price!)
- **Objection handling:** Rehearsed, scripted responses to counter every customer objection, at time of offer, and close sales despite reservations. May also involve high-pressure tactics like a false sense of scarcity or urgency. ("This offer expires in an hour!")
- **Emotion manipulation:** Uncover and play on a prospective client's fears and doubts to close a sale.

These tactics don't feel good to us as either sellers or consumers. With this kind of reputation, it's no wonder so many of us have a real aversion to selling and to feeling we are being sold to.

I speak to hundreds of small business owners every month, and I see the connection between these outdated sales tactics and the number of small businesses that fail.

Today's consumers are smarter, more informed, more discerning and more demanding than ever before. There has to be a fundamental shift in how to sell. This book isn't a replacement rulebook; it's not a blueprint or a paint by numbers approach. We all know business is more nuanced than that. There isn't only one way to do things. What works for me may not work for you.

Instead, it is a series of principles and ideas to adapt to your own style. Trial, test, tweak, refine and repeat them to become wildly successful at sales on your own terms.

I have a long history of not playing by the (sales) rules and can happily report after twenty-five years that it hasn't done my business any harm! (At least, not when those rules make no sense and are no longer fit for purpose in today's world.)

If it doesn't make sense and if it doesn't feel good, I'm not doing it. Regardless of what everyone else seems to be saying or doing.

- **1996** - Walked out of my first telesales job at eighteen years old within ninety minutes. I'd have left sooner but didn't want to cause a scene so left quietly on tea break and got the bus home, mortified and swearing I'd never work in sales again.

- **2000** - Worked in sales but got into trouble early on. I was smashing my financial targets and was the top performing consultant, but I wasn't achieving my recommended cold call or sales meeting numbers – because I believed in quality over quantity and qualification of leads.

- **2007** - Shunned the stilettos, shiny suits, egos and the very busy, very important Blackberry-using ego in favour of jeans, flip flops and work from the beach vibes, but making three times the sales of a lot of the successful UK expats buzzing about on the recruitment scene in Sydney. (Success without the ego and the bragging is possible!)

- **2008** - Co-founded a recruitment company because on my return to Scotland I was so appalled by the lack of integrity and vision in the recruitment industry when it came to sales and client experience. I didn't want to work for anyone else.

- **2017** - Applied everything I had learned in business to growing my children's activity business even though my competitors grumbled I was too sales-y and it would never work in children's activities. (It did and it does. Competitors now quite regularly copycat our marketing.)

- **2020 to present** - Helping other entrepreneurs rip up the tired, dated old rulebook of selling to create sales success in a way that works for them and their clients.

My twenty-five years (and counting) career in sales and business development has been incredibly fun and rewarding. I've had many opportunities and experiences. Most importantly I have made connections with remarkable people who do brilliant things.

My ability to sell has taken me around the world with clients across five continents. I've won £1 million+ contracts with international governments, I've recruited flying doctors for Outback Australia, I've built and sold out a baby swim school for local parents and I've sold consultancy and mentoring to hundreds of businesses (and a whole lot more in between!)

I haven't been hindered by refusing to play by these outdated and sometimes arbitrary rules when it comes to sales. I believe my refusal to play by these rules is exactly why I have succeeded. I want you to have success, freedom and amazing opportunities too.

I am on a mission to help you find the way to sell that suits you. When it comes to business, it is ok to zig, even when everyone else is telling you to zag. You don't need anyone's permission to build your business in the way that feels right for you.

This book tells you everything I have learned about sales. It's the good, the bad and the ugly, with no holds barred... and no gatekeeping of knowledge. This book isn't a prelude to get you to sign up for an expensive course. I have poured everything into it and I honestly want you to use it to help you make more sales and change the trajectory of your business (and your impact and earnings!)

But before we get started, it is important that I outline two things.

Firstly, there are no magic pills, silver bullets or success secrets in business despite what a lot of people might try to sell. Success takes hard work, fortitude, tenacity, smarts, self-awareness and the commitment to keep going, one foot in front of the other, even when times get tough. Boring but true – but you're smart, you already knew that. In fact, most people know that, despite the shiny marketing of the new miracle secrets out there. (Wealth codes, anyone?!)

Secondly, we think of success as making money, growing our business, and creating freedom. But even after all that, real success comes in the ability to do all of this *and* to live a life you love, surrounded by people you love, to be true to yourself, to build positive relationships, to be transparent and to keep your word and feel pride and enjoyment in all you do. That is when you are truly successful.

The principles I teach can be applied to selling anything. But I want to point out that some things are not for sale. Not ever. For me, that's my principles, my integrity, my values, my peace of mind and my relationships. These are sacred. And although I can sell (and have sold) a lot of things, I will never sell my soul.

I will only sell what I wholeheartedly believe in and you should too.

With Love,

Anna x

Part 1
Introducing The VALUE Sales Method:

So many people tell me *'I'm not good at sales'*. They don't present it as a skills gap or an area they are improving, they present it as a fixed state, a characteristic, just part of who they are. Let's clear that up: **No one is born good at sales.** And being good at sales isn't a genetically pre-defined permanent state in the way that we are born with blue eyes or brown eyes, or able to roll our tongue or not. Your ability to sell is not binary or fixed. It is a skill which you can learn.

As an entrepreneur you have to learn how to do a lot of things; code websites, VAT returns, manage staff and suppliers, create Instagram reels... the list goes on. Most of these tasks are things you did not know how to do or even really consider when you set up a business to follow your passion, but you do them because they are essential parts of entrepreneurship. So is sales; in fact, it is the key part because everything you want in your business and your life lies on the other side of making sales. So commit to learning how to make more sales the right way, and in a way that feels really good.

Sales is a process, a science, a series of steps, and just like driving a car or baking a cake, it can be learned. Sure, it might be a bit clunky the first time you follow the steps, but keep repeating the steps and become more familiar, and you'll get better every time. In the end, your sales process will feel as natural as riding a bike or driving a car and it will be woven into everything you do.

When you get to the stage when each part of your business is underpinned by your sales strategy, all the tasks work together like cogs in a machine to amplify your results.

Based on all that I have learned about how to create more sales, I have created the VALUE method as a framework to guide my clients, and now you, through the steps of a successful sales strategy.

The VALUE Method:

The **VALUE** Method is a five-step process based on the client journey. You can employ it in any industry or setting (I am yet to find one where it doesn't apply!) to generate consistent sales and build momentum in your business.

The five steps work together to support each other and create the optimum conditions for you to make sales.

A lot of the time we think about selling as a specific point in time when we say *buy this thing* or *click here* – the specific micro-moment of asking someone to buy. But, sales isn't just one moment in time. It should actually be a journey and an experience, and a time where you build trust and build relationships with your prospective clients over a period of time, so that the sale becomes inevitable because your process is designed that way.

Consider:

- Before the sale
- At the time of the sale
- After the sale

When you stop thinking about it as one micro-moment, one chance, one all-or-nothing point in time, and start considering it as a client journey, crafted so that it becomes inevitable that someone buys at some point, then you can really build a successful process, optimised for sales.

Follow this five-part VALUE Sales process, work through each of these five steps, and commit to implement, review, refine and repeat with consistency, and you *will* make more sales.

* * *

Vision: Define your goals and set targets for a clear, focused approach.

Audience: Get visible with a clear, compelling message to build your audience.

Lead Generation: Take daily action to generate and nurture leads.

Unlock sales: Make compelling offers and convert leads into sales.

Excellence: Deliver with excellence and leverage your success.

* * *

How Does It Work?

Being good at 'sales' isn't about focusing your energy on just one moment in time. It's not just that one moment when you ask people to buy from you, or book now, or click a button, or enter their card number. Nor is the one task of selling distinct from all the other tasks you do in your business.

It is a process, and a series of steps. Each of these distinct stages can be refined and optimised for sales. At each step of the client journey, your job is to help that client move smoothly along to the next stage of the client journey.

When carried out correctly, each step supports the next and they work as cogs in your well-oiled sales machine, where the collective whole is more than the sum of its parts.

The more you put in at the beginning, the more success you will have at the end. But each step needs careful attention. A person who launches into trying to unlock sales without doing any of the groundwork (skipping to the U in VALUE) will have very limited success (if any). Similarly, someone who works hard to build and engage an audience but never makes offers or focuses on converting (getting stuck on the V and A of VALUE) will have a trickle of sales rather than a flow. These errors will lead you to only fulfil a fraction of your sales potential.

Each VALUE step is vitally important. When you put them all into action they will form the basis of your sales success and your business growth. This book will help you delve into each of these steps with simple actionable strategies. If you are impatient for results and keen to get started, here's what's coming.

Process overview

- **Vision:** Start with creating a powerful **Vision** of what you want to create and achieve, both in terms of external impact and also in terms of the level of income you want to achieve to support or unlock the lifestyle you really want. Dream big. Your vision should excite you. It should be so meaningful and purposeful that it supercharges your motivation, excitement levels, resilience and tenacity. With that powerful vision as your end goal, break it down into a series of SMART goals. These are stepping stones which will bridge the gap between where you are right now and where you want to be.
- **Audience:** Consider who you want to help and who you want to work with. Understand them, their wants and needs, the language they use, and what they

truly value. Create powerful, compelling messaging to convey what you do and speak to their greatest wants and needs to attract their attention, build an **audience**, and construct a visibility strategy that gets you showing up in front of them consistently.

- **Lead Generation:** Building an audience alone is not enough to make sales. Generate **leads** from that audience. These are people or organisations who either overtly or subtly give us a sign that they are interested in working with you. This can be done in many ways, including content that gets them to somehow raise their hand: conversations, events, free offers, low cost offers, direct outreach or invitation, advertising, etc.

- **Unlock Sales:** A lot of people stop at visibility or perhaps a bit of lead generation and do *OK* (ish) but need to take it up a notch to perform at a higher level. Your next job is to **unlock sales** by focusing on converting leads to clients. This is all about starting conversations, offering solutions, making compelling offers, following up to convert your leads to sales, and moving these people along to the next stage of the client journey.

- **Excellence at Point of Delivery:** When a lead becomes a paying client, deliver with **excellence**. Always. Most business owners are good at this but the vital, business boosting part they miss is leveraging this into upsells, follow-on products, alumni offers, subscriptions or repeat sales, retaining the client for the long term and increasing the lifetime value. Leverage your quality and excellence to gain good quality referrals, reviews and case studies. This brings more people into steps one, two and three of the process.

Look ahead and imagine you are three to six months into implementing the strategies in this book.

- You have a huge vision that excites and inspires you to action. It helps you keep going and feel motivated and excited even when things are tough.
- You have turned this powerful vision into really specific goals and actions which keep you moving forward with clarity. Everything you do is focused on results.
- You are consistently visible to reach new people every day. People pay attention because you have a compelling message.
- You are also learning and refining and getting better at everything you do. Not only do you bring more people into the top of your sales funnel, you convert more of them into clients.
- Your existing clients stay with you. They are loyal because you deliver.
- They also refer people and continually recommend you so you bring in more new clients.
- Then even more people champion your work, buy from you on repeat and bring others into your world.

Over time this client journey develops pace and momentum. It creates significant growth for your business.

Quick Wins

While you build out the longer-term strategy, you can usually create some quick wins too. Train yourself to always look for the low-hanging fruit, the easy opportunities, while you work on your longer-term strategy.

There are limited ways to grow your income. Which of the following give you the biggest opportunity for growth? Which levers can you pull to create better results quickly?

1. Increase your prices so the average sale value increases. Most entrepreneurs wildly undercharge.
2. Increase one person's average purchase. Upsell additional products and services or offer VIP/luxury upgrade options.
3. Increase the number of people you sell to. Bring new people in through marketing.
4. Increase people's buying frequency. Rebook appointments before the client leaves. Offer a loyalty scheme or other incentives to come back.

No matter how stuck you feel right now when it comes to sales, if you love what you do, care about your clients, and are passionate about your business, sales can feel natural and easy, and you can become very good at it.

Excited to apply the steps of the VALUE method to your business? Me too!

* * *

Exercise:

- Score yourself out of five for each step in the VALUE framework. Give yourself zero if you do nothing at all in this area and five if you are an expert level operator.
- Where are your most obvious opportunities for improvement?
- What can you implement straight away to make the quickest wins?
- What would you like to implement over a longer period?

* * *

Chapter 1
Why Sales Matter

There is an epidemic of failure in the entrepreneurial community.

And it is deadly.

- Twenty percent of small businesses in the UK will fail in the first year.
- Sixty percent will fail by year three.
- Only twenty-five percent survive fifteen years in business.

The reason for this is simple. A business can be everything you want in terms of impact, reward, freedom, success, and money, but your success hinges on your ability to create consistent revenue. This means... sales!

Sales are the heartbeat that keeps your business alive.

If your business doesn't have that heartbeat, you will become one of these statistics.

I don't want that for you or for any entrepreneur brave enough to set up a business and create something of their own.

Learning how to sell is the key to your success and to everything you want.

When you master the process of making sales on repeat, the opportunities and results keep coming and your business reaches that wonderful point where everything seems to come together. More people want to work with you than you could have imagined. You have to work out how to scale and you might need to bring in more help. You can charge a premium for what you do, you earn what you want to earn and choose the opportunities you take. Success starts to feel effortless; business feels easy. After months and years of hard work, other people suddenly see you as an overnight success!

* * *

Making Sales Means...

→ Revenue coming in and your business earning you money.

→ Creating impact and helping more people who need what you do.

→ You get to do what you love and create success on your terms.

Sales = Success + Impact + Income + Freedom

* * *

On the other hand, if you are not making sales or not making them frequently enough to be comfortable, you will be in struggle mode.

A lack of control over the flow of sales and revenue into your business will keep you stuck, broke and having little impact or fun. It leads to self-doubt, working for free, working with non-ideal clients, crazy offers, price reductions, long hours and sleepless nights. You feel like you are doing all the things, and working all the hours, but no matter what you do, you can't seem to get any traction.

But here's the good news. If you are in that struggle mode right now, a sales strategy is your fastest route out of it. Or if you already do OK (or even pretty well) without a sales strategy, imagine how much better you will do once you implement a sales strategy!

Wherever you start from, a sales strategy that delivers results can only improve your situation.

The stakes are high, then. Your ability to make sales and your control over the flow of sales can be the biggest indicator of your success *or* a potentially fatal roadblock on your way to success.

So why aren't we all raving about the wonders of sales and telling ourselves about the fantastic opportunity to change our fortunes and achieve all we desire? A sales strategy is the most fundamental part of a successful business, but most business owners I speak to don't have a cohesive sales strategy. Many even feel a real aversion to sales.

Sales has a bad name. When I meet people for the first time and tell them I am a sales expert, I see them giving me trepidatious sideways looks, worried about making eye contact in case I am about to launch into an awkward pitch. Sometimes people say it out loud: *oh, wow, you seem really nice and normal. I can't believe you are in sales!* Sometimes they look a bit sheepish and tell me: *I know I need to be doing sales but I just can't. It feels awkward and I don't want to look desperate.* Or they give a nervous laugh and say: *I probably need your help...*

This aversion to sales, this knowledge and skills gap, chokes so many small businesses before they can even begin. It kills their potential and their future.

That is a tragedy. It is a tragedy for the entrepreneurs whose dreams don't come to fruition and a tragedy for their potential clients who need what they offer but don't know about it. It is such a waste of potential and opportunity. If that is happening to you right now, I am sorry that is going on for you. It sucks to feel stuck in your business like that or to know you have untapped potential and you are missing out.

Together, we are going to fix it. We can fix it because I know exactly why it's happening.

Everything you have been taught about sales is wrong (*probably). Deep down, you might already know that too.

Chapter 2

Everything You've Been Taught About Sales Is Wrong* (*Probably)

Let's explore that idea. Most small business owners I meet have invested in some sort of sales training. They might have worked with a sales coach or trainer, or downloaded free trainings, attended masterclasses, joined boot camps, accelerators, courses, containers, masterminds, or group programmes.

There are programmes on how to close more sales, scripts teaching you to sell in the DMs, guides to help you book more discovery calls, challenges to convert those calls, scripts on how to handle common objections so you get the sale, lists of keywords to use or not use. The array of options out there is mind boggling and they all say they will help small business owners make more sales.

Maybe you've invested in that kind of thing.

Bought the scripts or prompts? Taken the course? Attended a workshop? Paid for someone's blueprint, the one-size-fits-all guaranteed solution to your sales challenges? There is a big problem with this. One size does *not* fit all.

If you value deep relationships and open communication, scripts will never feel good. If you've ever tried to use one of these copy-and-paste scripts, you know how awkward, robotic and far from a good client experience they are. If you value honesty and integrity, pushy sales tips won't feel good at all. If you are a quiet introvert, you won't show up in the same way that a high-energy, all-singing, all-dancing extrovert does.

Training is often based on just that: One person, using one method, getting one result, one time, but making money forevermore by selling that system. It isn't fit for purpose and it leaves the individual who has purchased it even more stuck when it comes to making sales and even less confident than they were before, wondering if it is a 'them' problem.

* * *

One Size Does Not Fit All...

There is no secret. There is no one-size-fits-all. Markets change. Someone creating one result one way doesn't mean you'll replicate it by repeating their tactic.

Tactic One: A yoga teacher had a fairly small and fairly new business when the pandemic hit in 2020. She moved her classes online quickly and then leveraged that success by teaching other yoga teachers how to do the same. By charging the other yoga teachers a premium she made

$10,000 a month. Now she sells a system that is her blueprint, based purely on helping all business owners make $10k months by selling a high ticket offer. But what worked in that very specific time in 2020 no longer works for her or her clients.

Tactic Two: At the beginning of my online journey, when email marketing was very new to me, a well-known coach hooked me in with *'The email sequence that made me £100k from my list of less than 500 people'*. Intriguing, right? It was to me, the new online business owner with an email list of fewer than five hundred people! But I was disappointed in 2021 when I received those emails and quickly saw they were very basic, sent on the back of her live events and getting face to face with people, just inviting people to book a discovery call with her.

They were created in 2016 when the market was radically different and way less sophisticated. There were fewer coaches, way less social media and less email marketing. What worked for her then doesn't work for anyone now. But it's still being sold as a one-size-fits-all. And I checked – it's still being used in her marketing now in 2023.

I'm not sharing these tactics to be negative. I'm not in the habit of attacking other business owners, and I believe to each their own.

However, if something is harmful to people and to a community I care about (and am part of), I think we need to call out and uncover some of these practices. I believe these types of trainings are not only a waste of your time and money, but are genuinely harmful, and there is too much of it going on in our wildly unregulated online world where anyone can declare themselves an expert on anything.

* * *

Even Once You Get Past That, There's Another Problem...

A lot of commonly taught sales training isn't designed around a great client experience. There is no long-term thinking or drive to build longevity into people's client relationships through quality.

It prioritises short-term wins over long-term relationships, focusing solely on getting the sale at all costs. This perpetuates the story that sales is about that one moment in time when we ask for card details, say *book now* or *buy my thing* rather than a long-term client journey. It teaches that sales success comes from forcing, pushing, persuading or manipulating our clients into buying from us rather than laying the groundwork, building trust, making relevant and compelling offers and then delivering with excellence.

The manipulation tactics being taught, the smoke and mirrors, the hard close, and the *never take no for an answer* approach are dated and ridiculous but still being sold, in some cases with a healthy side order of gas-lighting people into buying. You know how. *If you can't even find $5000 to pay for this training that is going to change your life, you clearly aren't serious about your business or your success. Frankly, I'm not going to force you as I don't waste my time* *with people who aren't positive and committed to their own success. Put it on a credit card.*

Even worse: *get into the vibration of receiving by investing in yourself and paying in full. How can you attract high-paying clients if you aren't one yourself?*

Sadly, this is not a joke. This sales tactic has been used far too often.

If you have invested time and money to learn about sales but feel disillusioned, disappointed, and more stuck than ever before, you are not alone. Many people come to me after investing thousands of pounds in things sold as high ticket sales programmes but have learned nothing or next to nothing that is actionable. They leave with only the credit card debt that they put the programme on.

Then they come to me and say *I know I need to do it but I hate selling; I don't even know where to start.* When something feels uncomfortable, and out of integrity with how we want to show up and interact, we won't do it. Every instinct tells us no.

* * *

The Client Experience No One Wants...

I invested in a sales coach early in my journey into this online world. I had over twenty years of experience in sales and entrepreneurship, but selling on social media and using funnels were newer to me. In our first session, he told me to put out a post to say I was giving away ten free one-hour coaching sessions. They were going to be mind blowing and life changing and if people wanted one they should comment on my post and I would select the winners.

He gave me a script to use on the calls which was all about uncovering these people's pain points. This was to sell a one-to-one mentoring offer that cost several thousand pounds, not a cheap spur of the moment purchase. In his words, I had to 'press hard' on the pain points to close the sale. He wanted me to record the calls so he could critique them and help me refine my process.

I just could not. It was wrong on so many levels.

- It was not a giveaway, it was a sales pitch. The relationships would have started with a lie.
- No one was getting coaching. I was supposed to uncover their biggest vulnerabilities then use them to manipulate them into paying me.
- I was to do these calls with clients who hadn't been pre-qualified on price/readiness to invest, which is a waste of everyone's time.
- I would have quickly burned through the goodwill and relationships I had spent years building up in my network.

This is where I parted company with this coach. I told him I thought his tactics were wrong on many levels. He (of course) told me it was a 'me' issue: I was blocking myself from success; I had a mindset issue, maybe linked to child-hood trauma(?!), and a fear of success. He suggested I should meditate six times a day, work on my money mindset, and also work out daily to lose weight because I'd be more successful if I wasn't perceived as lazy or undisciplined due to being overweight. I mean... *wow*. So much to unpack there.

I keep seeing this tired old tactic on social media. Today, while writing, close to the end of 2023, I have seen two separate connections of mine post it, using *exactly* the same script. It is very much on my mind.

Let's just stop. There are many more effective ways to get leads that don't leave you feeling like you need a shower afterwards. Not only does it lack integrity, it makes you *look* disingenuous and actually repels clients so it is not even effective.

If something feels wrong, you get to say no. *You* get to call the shots.

As a side note, when you have a good sales strategy, you will be so busy with paying clients that there is no way you'll spend ten hours of your time speaking with completely unqualified prospects on the off chance you can pressure them into a sale.. You will be far too busy serving your paying clients and engaging with your qualified leads to waste time like that.

More on your lead generation and prospect qualification process later in this book. (You'll find this in Part Four if you want to dive ahead)

* * *

I've been in sales for twenty-five years. I know my stuff, I know the stakes, and I know what business success entails. I have the security and validation of my sales career to look back on. I know when to tell someone I disagree with them, and that there is a better way to do business and make sales. But most entrepreneurs and small business owners don't have a sales background to give them that certainty. They get sucked in by this nonsense.

That is why I am so passionate about spreading the word that this old-school approach to sales *does not work*. It not only wastes your time, it also leaves you worse off than you were before. It damages your reputation and client relation-ships, and dents your confidence, leaving you feeling like it's a 'you' problem, like you're not enough, like you can't succeed.

It's not a you problem. It's an industry problem, a hangover from the bad old days of sleazy sales and patriarchal capi-talism when no one cared about the customers. It's actively harms the small business and entrepreneurial community.

Let's say enough is enough. No more scripts, secrets, one size fits all, fake scarcity, fake urgency, secret offers, FOMO marketing, trauma marketing, bro-marketing, girl-bossing, manifesting money with wealth codes, paying exorbitant amounts for poor quality coaching and all the other bad practices that have been prevalent.

No more sales coaching that doesn't prioritise longevity and client experience. Let's call time on all of it.

Let's rip up the rulebook of selling, and stop subscribing to these tactics that simply make a few people rich while keeping more entrepreneurs stuck than successful.

Let's change the way you think about sales in your business.

Are you with me? Good. So the old way is out. What's the new way?

The Paradigm Shift (Where the Client Comes First)

This is where it gets exciting. A paradigm shift is happening right now in the world of sales. Consumers are wiser and smarter than ever before. They are more informed and have access to so much information in a few taps on their phone. They have higher standards and want more: they want authenticity, personalisation and value. Most of all they want integrity. They want to be listened to, heard and understood and to have the right solutions compellingly presented to them.

People don't want to be told or talked at, to be pushed into something they don't want or charmed into buying some-thing they don't need. People who sell this way *might* make some short-term wins and quick cash, but they won't build long-lasting relationships with their clients. They won't prioritise excellence in their delivery. They will quickly burn through a lot of clients, get into a lot of payment disputes, and burn their reputation as well, which is an exhausting way to do business. It is so much easier, rewarding and lucrative to play the long game. Focus your attention on building lasting relationships that benefit both parties for years to come. Create win-win scenarios for you and your clients so buying from you is an easy yes.

I have read a lot of sales books. One misguided gem describes the pause after you say the price on a discovery call as the *winner's pause*. Whoever speaks first is the loser. This book instructs the reader to make sure the client speaks first. I don't see closing a sale and starting a new client relationship in that way. I do not describe someone buying from me as a loser! I want it to be a positive, empowered buying decision: a win-win.

Success needs a smart sales process. Sales has to be about long-term thinking, building relationships, being a person of value, being trustworthy, and acting with integrity.

All this is a huge opportunity. As an entrepreneur and small business owner, this is where you can be very strong. You can think big in terms of goals and vision, but you can also build relationships and interact with real personal connection and client proximity. Also, you can be agile enough to recognise and respond quickly to market trends and client needs, and adapt and evolve your way to success.

That shift to selling in a way that places the customer at the centre of all you do, based on trust and relationships and delivering with integrity, is what this book is all about. I have always worked this way and it is without doubt the number one reason why I am successful. (The number two reason is an absolute refusal to give up on things. I keep trying until something works!)

Key Takeaways:

- You have to be able to sell your stuff. It's not optional. If you are an entrepreneur or business leader you need to be able to sell.
- To do that you need a sales strategy that works for you *and* your clients.
- There is no one size fits all solution. There *is* a series of steps and principles that will help you develop a sales strategy that feels good for you and your clients.
- *You* get to design the sales process that works for you. You are a good person, doing great things with integrity so your sales process should reflect that and feel positive for all involved.

Your Action Steps:

- Consider how you feel about sales. How actively you are selling right now?
- Note where you feel resistance or are holding back. Consider why.
- Think of times you have been a client or potential client. Think about both good and bad experiences you have had of being sold to. Make some notes. What felt good? What didn't? What can you learn from that experience? How can you use that learning to enhance your own process?

Chapter 3

Sales Success Is Possible for Everyone

Before we move on, we should address the elephants in the room.

Let's call Elephant One Nelly. You might be thinking, *It's alright for you: you must be a natural at sales*. I can assure you that no one is born good at sales. It is a process to learn just like any other process. I am not even what you might think of as your typical sales expert. I'm an introvert, I'm quite shy in many ways, I like to be liked, and I am absolutely allergic to pushy or manipulative sales tactics.

Despite not fitting the 'typical' profile of a sales coach, I am very good at selling because I found the way that suits me. I don't try to 'fix' my weaknesses, or fake it till I make it, or adopt a different persona to sell. I lean into my strengths and do what I am truly good at (and love doing) to create sales. And you can too.

Elephant Two. You are probably wondering, *will this book work for me?* You might feel you or your business has a unique aspect that makes it unlikely it will work for you.

I often hear:

'Will it work for me and my business if/because (insert some perfectly normal thing).'

Short answer: Yes.

Slightly longer answer: If you implement what you learn, review your progress, and tweak and refine it, and commit to doing all of this consistently, then yes, this will work for you.

Whether you are selling products or services, whether you are online or offline, whether you are business to business or business to consumer, whether you are high ticket or low ticket, whether you are full-time or part-time, if you work around family or caring responsibilities, if you have ambitions so big they scare you, if you are neurodiverse, if you are an introvert, if you live with chronic illness... or whatever else you are wondering about, no matter how stuck you feel right now when it comes to sales... Yes! Yes! Yes! This will work for you.

If you are at the beginning of your journey and not making many sales at all, this book will help you create that first flow of sales. If you are already making some sales, this process will help you dial up those results and make many more sales.

I know that because these principles have helped me build three wildly successful but incredibly different businesses from the ground up and helped my clients with completely different businesses.

Sales is fundamentally about relationships and about solving problems for people and when we commit to solving our clients' problems, we make sales.

This book is about you, not me, but you might be wondering who I am to be telling you about sales. Am I qualified to give you advice?

My sales career began in 1999, selling boat trips to tourists on the island of Crete. My first professional sales job was working in recruitment in 2000, although I took my first recruitment job on the proviso that I would never do sales. I was an account manager, not a new business developer.

I was a good account manager but within two or three months I could see my peers earning bonuses that doubled or tripled their salaries. They were celebrated as big success stories because they were bringing in new business. I worked hard, I knew I was good at what I did, and I wanted a bit of that kudos, the recognition, the excitement of new sales... and yes, the money that would fund my girl about town lifestyle!

And all I had to do was find new clients? I could definitely do that, I thought. And I did. I quickly became top biller there, which was the start of a sixteen-year career in recruitment, the last nine spent as Managing Director and Cofounder of an international agency where I created multi-six figure sales in year one, and went on to grow that business to a team of twenty-five staff, multi-seven figure revenue and clients across five continents.

After I'd had my children, in quite quick succession, I realised the international travel, the long hours, the calls in different time zones, leading a big sales team, and reporting to a board just wasn't what I wanted anymore. Being off with my second baby gave me a taste of being at home with both kids. I desperately wanted to continue that, so it was time for a change.

Getting another job wasn't an option. I knew that wouldn't give me the freedom and flexibility or the earnings I needed.

So, I exited that business early in 2017 with a six-month-old baby, a toddler and a slightly wild idea, but with the confidence that I would make it work. I went from Managing Director of an international executive recruitment consultancy to starting my own baby swim school, competing against the big franchises. I built a new business in a brand new industry, as a solo founder with 100% control. I hired my first team members four months in, and by the end of year one had built a small team and created six-figure sales. This family business still exists seven years later, although I am much more removed from the daily operations (the team do everything much better than I can!), serving over seven hundred customers a week and growing month on month.

When I set up the swim business, I got involved in local networking and entrepreneurial communities and found they were packed with women just like me. I loved the connection and support. But as my business grew rapidly more and more people asked me how I'd grown so quickly and what the secret was.

I saw just how many brave, brilliant entrepreneurs out there were trying to create a better life for themselves through a business, but struggled due to a lack of sales and marketing knowledge. Their lack of sales success was eroding their overall business confidence. I realised how much I enjoyed helping people with ideas. After years of leading a business, I had a real knack for spotting gaps and opportunities in other people's businesses, understanding what people needed to do to make their businesses successful, and helping them believe in themselves too.

People asked to take me for coffee and pick my brains, asked me to speak at networking, and asked more and more often if I would coach them. I had never seen myself as a coach, but I knew I could help and impact them, and how much people wanted and needed that help. I also knew how much I enjoyed it. In late 2018, I set up my business mentoring business, which has evolved into what it is today.

After that quick history, I hope you feel you are in safe hands with me.

What is most important to take from all of this is not my CV or my suitability to guide you in this journey towards more sales, but to look beyond that and see the range of industries and businesses I have been in. Whether negotiating a million-pound recruitment contract with the Qatari government, recruiting flying doctors for outback Australia, or selling a £47.50 swimming lesson subscription to a local parent, the same principles applied.

These principles have helped so many of my incredible and long-standing clients in the following professions to sell more too. I've helped photographers, artists, designers, social media managers, coaches, education providers, nurseries, a nanny agency, sleep consultants, creatives, accountants, forest schools, course creators, crafters, candle makers, architects, yogis, psychologists, dentists, therapists, training academies, children's activity providers, nutritionists, business coaches, academic institutions, marketing consultants, copywriters, web designers, writers, vets, party planners, life coaches, retailers, app developers, academics, therapists, beauty business owners, financial coaches, designers, dressmakers, PTs, health coaches, parenting experts, consultants, community managers, gift companies, subscription boxes, recruitment agencies, a sex therapist, PR consultants and agency owners, podcasters, luxury brands, bookkeepers, menopause coaches, training academies, food and drinks brands...

I am sure there are quite a few clients that haven't been included in this list. Every business is different but the same sales principles and the same commitment to action and consistency have helped them to thrive.

I know they will work for you too.

Chapter 4
Sales Confidence

When I ask people to describe how sales makes them feel they use words like *awkward, shy, embarrassed.* Sometimes people say they feel fearful or they have a physical reaction and they feel sick or shaky at the idea of selling.

How would you feel if I asked you to go and sell something right now? Nervous? Excited? Ready? Awkward and unsure?

Let's flip that and reframe it to see selling as a hugely positive means to an end in that it is your way to connect deeply with clients, to succeed while doing the thing you love, and to achieve your big goals. That is worth getting excited about, right?

It is normal to want to stay safe, avoid pain, disappointment, rejection, and embarrassment. We must start with our own minds and reframe our beliefs about sales and about rejection so these become more minor issues. We also need to detach from the individual outcomes and focus more on the big goal.

That is a staged process:

1. Reframe selling as something positive.
2. Detach from the individual outcomes.
3. Understand how your sales activity is directly linked with your bigger result and use that for resilience.

Reframe Selling as Something Positive

First of all, recognise what comes up for you when you think of sales. Any negative associations? I've had people tell me they feel it's cringeworthy, desperate, embarrassing, pushy... or even that it feels greedy or immoral. Do you have any unconscious biases or negative associations like this?

You are in charge of the sales process and you get to create whatever experience you want for your clients so you can make it a hugely positive experience. If you are an ethical person with integrity, your sales process won't be anything other than that. So, let's reframe any negative beliefs. What belief are you harbouring? What is the opposite of this negative belief? Or what workaround can you find?

I don't even think of sales or selling as a distinct activity, it is just woven through almost every task I do in my business. It is listening, asking questions, offering solutions and asking if you can help people. I am super-clear on the value I offer and the impact I can have, so I get excited about how many more people I can help and what results we can achieve together. The act of selling feels just like talking about something I am passionate about, to people I like, telling them (with their permission) how I can help them and asking them if they'd like my help.

So rather than selling it is talking, listening, telling, serving, helping... What works for you to reframe sales to something that feels better? Helping? Telling? Serving?

Next...

Detach From the Outcome

When you ask someone if they'd like to buy your thing, what's the worst that can happen? That someone will say no? Let's get clear on that from the beginning. This is always going to happen at some point as no one has a one hundred percent close rate.

Stop worrying about the possible nos and get excited about all the possible yeses you are going to hear. Do your best and know that for every person who says no, there will be others who say yes.

When you do get a no, ask yourself whether there is an opportunity to learn anything, refine your process, better qualify a prospective client, and be more informative in your content. Sometimes there will be and sometimes there won't. To succeed you need the resilience to keep going, keep asking and know that if you keep repeating the process and refuse to stop you can never fail, you will just learn and improve and then you will succeed.

Detach from each individual outcome. Stay focused on the bigger task. Lots of people try once or twice and give up because they don't make instant sales. What a pity and what a waste. When I first started online I found it incredibly helpful to learn about the huge online success stories whose books I was reading and courses I was buying. I learned how one person's first launch was a flop, and how someone else only sold three of their programmes, yet they went on to make multi-millions. My big takeaway was, they didn't stop. They figured it out and you can too.

There's a school of thought in entrepreneurship that if you aren't failing regularly then you are playing it too safe and too small. The best and most successful business owners fail regularly because they dream big and try new ideas, and they know how to fail *well*. Fail fast and fail cheap; learn and go again is some of the best entrepreneurial advice I've ever been given.

When you have more experience you'll start to know your own conversion rates. Perhaps five percent of website visitors make a purchase; ten percent buy when you run a free challenge to launch something; seventy percent of discovery calls convert and over thirty days that increases to eighty-five percent. But you won't know these until you get to work And once you've established them you can improve them.

I cannot guarantee you will make a sale every time you try to sell. But I can guarantee that you will make more sales than if you don't try to sell.

"You miss one hundred percent of the shots you don't take."

— Michael Jordan

If you take no sales action, you get no results. Nor do you get data about why your sales process is or isn't working. If you take no action, you are guaranteed a negative outcome. If you take action, you cannot help but create some kind of positive outcome. Even the worst-case scenario is testing your offer in the market and getting feedback that will help you refine it.

Whatever it is that you do, selling is just how you can help more people and create more impact in the world, and it also gives you more financial freedom and security.

So get out of your own head, get out of your own way, and start feeling good about selling.

Negative Thoughts/Beliefs

What negative thoughts and beliefs come up for you when you think about selling? Do you wonder if you are capable of success? Do fear or doubt start to creep in? And trust me, ,Each time you hit a new level of success or are about to play on a whole bigger scale, that stuff can rear its head. I know it can, even when you think you have dealt with all of that mindset stuff. I have learned that getting out of my head and into action is the best way for me to quell those fears and doubts.

There are other great things you can do too:

1. **Look for evidence.** If you experience negative thoughts such as *I'm not good at this* or *nobody likes what I do*, ask if that is really true, or if it is just mind monkeys at work. Look for the evidence that supports the belief, then look for the evidence that disproves it. Collate everything. Weigh up the evidence and see what it tells you.
2. **Remind yourself of what you can do and have done.** I love to look at client successes and read old cards, emails and reviews thanking me for how I have helped them. My friend and I were chatting about this recently and she shared an excellent idea of having an 'I can' wall or pinboard where you stick photos, cards, and visual reminders of all you have achieved so that when you have a wobbly moment, looking at that 'I can' wall will take you right back to where you need to be.
3. **Remind yourself why you are doing this.** Why does this matter? What are you working towards?
4. **Keep going.** You've got this. The more you do, acting with courage, and proving to yourself that you can do things, the more you will build courage. Confidence comes from having the courage to act.

* * *

Reframing Guilt About Selling

Lots of people feel excited about earning lots of money. If that's you, brilliant. But it's not that easy for some people because of their background or the narrative they've heard about money throughout their lives.

Many of my clients, especially those who work in 'helping' professions, carry guilt or shame for wanting to make money. Of course, this means they hold back when it comes to selling and to having money conversations. But it is entirely reasonable to help *and* to get paid well. The two do not have to be incompatible.

One of my incredible clients, Dina, is an anxiety specialist who helps young people when anxiety causes them to avoid school and affects their education. Dina is a lovely, kind, caring person and has worked for charities and not-for-profits most of her career. However, she is now a business owner now and needs to charge at a level which reflects the deep work she does and the time and resources that takes. Equality, fairness and accessibility are some of her core values. When we reviewed her pricing, it brought up guilt that some families wouldn't be able to afford her help.

A lot of people feel this guilt, especially in helping or caring businesses, and the default outcome is to keep all prices low which quite often keeps the business in struggle mode. That doesn't help anyone.

Instead Dina committed to four things:

1. A reframe that by charging a higher price, she would be able to grow a sustainable business with the resources to give back.
2. For every ten paying clients, she would give a free place to a family who otherwise would not be able to access her one-to-one support.
3. A low-cost digital bundle to support people at an extremely accessible price point.
4. Free resources and guides as well as regular tips, Q&As and support on social media, accessible to all.

Outcome: By growing a thriving business, Dina will be able to help more young people, many of whom would not otherwise be able to access support.

Takeaway: You can earn money and be a good person who does good things in the world. These identities are not mutually exclusive. Creating a successful business which earns money gives you much more opportunity to give back and to support people if that is what you want to do.

* * *

Homework

1. What is your reframe or new belief about sales?
2. What limiting or negative thoughts creep up on you and how can you counter these?

Chapter 5

Your Strengths Are Your Success

Use What You've Got to Create a Sales Process That Feels Natural

We are hard-wired for survival. Psychologically, we do not want to do things that make us feel bad and we will go to almost any lengths to avoid them. When you think of sales as something that makes your skin crawl, and your toes curl at the thought of interacting with your prospective clients in that way, I could bet my life on it that you won't do it. Not consistently and not well.

But here's the really good news: you don't have to do anything that doesn't feel right. In fact, the more aligned your sales process is to your personality and your approach, the more successful you will be. So first of all, know and believe with every fibre of your being that you can and will create maximum sales success when you sell in a way that is aligned with your personality, your ethos and your values.

Also, think about your greatest strengths, your personality type, and how you like to connect with people. Start to think about embracing your strengths and leaning into them more to help you achieve your goals, instead of focusing on your weaknesses and trying to fit a square peg into a round hole.

When you sell the right way for you, you won't feel awkward or embarrassed. You will feel like you have had the best day ever.

I have already told you that as a shy introvert, allergic to pushy or manipulative sales tactics, I'm not your 'typical' sales coach. I sell in the way that suits me and feels good. It makes me laugh when I get these cold pitches in my DMs promising to get me thirty to fifty qualified calls a week because I just think no, that is not how I want to spend my week! It is such a bad pitch. A diary full of discovery calls with people I don't know doesn't fill me with excitement.

I much prefer a relaxed approach. I love chatting to people individually or in small groups, I love sharing my knowledge and I love helping people figure out their next steps. Building relationships, making connections and selling in a consultative way works for me. This has always worked one-to-one, and as my business grows and scales, I can leverage these skills through speaking engagements, group training, videos, this book, podcasts, and my social media. They all lead with value and open up connection and conversation.

Let's talk about you. What are your core values? What are your strengths? How do you enjoy interacting with people? How can you leverage these strengths? How do you want your clients to feel when they engage with your business?

People won't always remember exactly what you said or exactly what happened, but they will remember how you made them feel. Make them feel the way you want all your clients to feel - for me that's valued, supported, appreciated, understood, and also empowered and excited about what may be possible.

* * *

Generosity in the Sales Process

Be generous, share your knowledge, give value, help people, recommend people, and connect people. I don't mean work for free, but when you can and it doesn't cost you anything you don't want to give, being generous works.

Give people appropriate advice, or arrange 'ask me anything' sessions or Q&As. Over-deliver, exceed their expectations and surprise people with extra touches or attention to detail. It not only feels great, it is the easiest way to get people to love what you do, love your business, remember you and talk positively about you too.

Some of my clients from years ago in different businesses and different industries still support me, recommend me and champion my business even though it's no longer relevant to them. It is because of the client experience I created and the relationship I made.

Generosity feels good. It also makes it natural and easy to sell. People already know, like and trust you if you have helped them.

* * *

Inject as much as you can of your own personality and values into the client experience and how you interact with people:

- If you are funny and humour is appropriate for your industry, use your sense of humour. Make humour part of your brand personality and client experience. Use humour in your marketing, comms and conversations.
- If you are spiritual, use that.
- If you are a rebel with a cause, use that.
- Love to travel? Show it.
- Obsessed with a quirky hobby or niche interest? Share it.

The more of **you** you put into the client experience, the more natural it will feel to build relationships and to help people along the journey from being a brand new connection to being a loyal and happy client.

* * *

The Psychology of Success

Strengths psychology is about finding what you're naturally good at and doing more of it.

It is part of the positive psychology field, which studies what is going right with people instead of what is going wrong, and uses those learnings to elevate individuals' happiness, success and wellbeing. Positive psychology gained traction in the early 2000s.

When it comes to strengths psychology, the key message is that we are at our most productive, successful and happy when we focus on developing our strongest skills, rather than fixing our weaknesses.

When you understand what your innate strengths are and you leverage them to get results in your sales process, you get the best outcomes. You are happier, more engaged, more natural, more productive and more successful.

Identifying and leveraging your strengths can mean the difference between a thriving business you love and a struggling business which feels like constant hard work. When it comes to sales, you can play to your unique strengths in how you connect with potential clients, how you engage and nurture relationships, how you convert them and how you go on to deliver with excellence. This can power up your results.

- **Strategy.** Knowing your strengths allows you to develop a sales strategy that feels natural to you, whether that's through storytelling if you're good at communication, analysis if you're data-driven, or relationships if you're a natural at relating to others' feelings.
- **Authenticity.** Salespeople who use their strengths will appear more natural, authentic and genuine, building trust and creating stronger relationships.

- **Efficiency.** When you work in a way that suits your strengths, you will be more efficient and effective. The work will feel natural and easy so you get more done in a shorter time.

So, identify and understand your strengths, your own specific zone of genius, the work you do that never feels like work, and when you are at your most productive. Build strategies that use these skills.

Consider how you can develop your strengths further and how you can use them even more to achieve your goals. Lean in.

If this is interesting to you and you'd like to know more, I recommend: the CliftonStrengths StrengthsFinder assessment online. For a fairly low fee, you can take the assessment and get a personalised report which will identify your unique skills and strengths.

Another really helpful (and free) psychological assessment tool online is The VIA Character Assessment, which helps people identify their character strengths. In simple terms, it's a quiz that uncovers what's best about you—things like kindness, bravery, creativity, or other positive traits.

When you read both reports you'll see that the combination of character strengths and 'doing' strengths are two sides of the same coin. You will likely recognise yourself very clearly, which can help you clarify your messaging, your brand and exactly what unique strengths you bring to the client experience.

By understanding your strengths and your positive traits, you can use them more in your professional life and in your sales process, to be happier and more successful.

* * *

Key Takeaways:

- When you do it right, selling should feel like the most natural thing in your business.
- Understand your own unique skills, strengths and values so you can leverage these to help you succeed.
- Use your natural strengths and inject your values, personality and ethos into your business to make sales feel way more easy and joyful.
- Take the CliftonStrengths assessment or the VIA Character assessment to learn more about yourself.

Part 2

Vision and Goals

Vision: Define your goals and set targets for a clear, focused approach.

Audience: Get visible with a clear, compelling message to build your audience.

Lead Generation: Take daily action to generate and nurture leads.

Unlock sales: Make compelling offers and convert leads into sales.

Excellence: Deliver with excellence and leverage your success.

Chapter 6
What Do You Really Want?

"Tell me, what is it you plan to do with your one wild and precious life?"

— Mary Oliver

The average human lifespan is around four thousand weeks. Life is short and life is precious. What wonderful things are you going to fill your weeks with?

We all want to enjoy life but it is also good to enjoy work. Don't grow a business that drains you and you need to take a holiday from. Grow a business that:

You love so much it never feels like work.

Is successful enough to unlock or support the lifestyle, experiences and security you really want.

It is time to get excited, to think about what is really possible for you. What do you want to do with this one precious life?

Don't worry about dreaming too big; worry instead about whether you are dreaming big enough. Dream big and use those dreams to create huge, meaningful goals. Then break those goals down into a series of action steps to take you all the way to where you want to go.

These steps, the mindset and positivity around selling, the creation of a big vision and linking that huge vision to meaningful, purposeful goals, these are the solid foundations on which you will build your sales success. You will get to the nitty gritty tactics soon enough, things like how to build a sales funnel or what to say to close a sale. First, though, build your foundations with the tasks in this chapter.

The What and the Why

Before you get to the how, let's think about the what and the why. Dig deep and examine what you really want, because unless you know what you want and why it's important, you can't know how to get there.

What do you really want to achieve in the next three to five years in your business? And in your life? If anything and everything is possible for you, what do you choose?

Then go deeper. Ask yourself:

- Why?
- What does that look like?

- Why does that matter?
- What does that mean?

You might have to go through a few layers of 'why' but that's what takes you to the root of it. (Parents who've been through the toddler years will be well versed in 'why' questioning. After several whys you get to the fundamental truth, even if it's just 'because it is'.) That's where you want to get to with layers of asking 'why' when figuring out what you really want – the fundamental truth.

Dream Big

Make your goals huge, audacious, perhaps even a little scary. They should excite you, motivate you and mean the world to you.

When your goals are meaningful, you are more motivated and more resilient, which is essential for overcoming obstacles and achieving success. Your goals and purpose will drive you forward even when the going gets tough.

We don't give up on the things that really matter to us. Most of us aren't motivated or inspired by cold hard cash in the bank. What matters is what that cash allows us to do.

If, for example, you want to achieve one million pounds in sales within the next five years, why is that? Is it so you can travel first class around the world? Buy your dream home? Start a charitable foundation? Buy a home for your child or your parents? Know that you can retire comfortably in the future? Buy designer handbags or a luxury car? Pay school fees? Install a swimming pool? You know what is meaningful and motivating to you so attach some meaning to that financial result.

There are two kinds of meaning and purpose: internal and external. The best, most compelling goals and visions combine them. The more purpose and meaning your goal has, the higher your chances of success.

Let's look closely at each type of meaning and purpose.

Meaning and Purpose One: Your Caveman Brain and Lifestyle Drivers

To return to our primitive caveman brains, which are hard-wired for survival and continually looking to satisfy our need to survive and thrive in the world, this is the *'what's in it for me'* part.

Your business has to meet your needs, and support or unlock the lifestyle you want for yourself and those you love. What does that lifestyle look like? What level of income do you need to unlock all that you want? Build out from there. If that's what you want to earn each month or year, what does that mean in terms of a sales goal for the business?

Your goals will change. As your business grows, your goals can grow with you. When you achieve one set of goals, dream bigger. You can believe more is possible.

Exercise

What do you really want to achieve? What would you love to be, do and have? Have fun with this. Write a wish list of twenty things you want (possessions, experiences, time, etc.) in a notebook and then get obsessed with ticking these off. Redo this once a year, in the same journal if you can. I have done this every year since 2018 and it is incredible to see that many items on my lists of hopes and dreams, which at the time seemed huge and out of reach, have come to fruition.

I like making a list and then ticking things off. It is very satisfying. Maybe you do this too? Perhaps you prefer a vision board or Pinterest board. You choose what works for you, but do it. Enjoy it.

My wish list is mainly about travelling and experiences, with a bit of home stuff. Others' lists comprise designer bags or shoes or fine dining... you choose. I love to know what my clients have on their lists. Sometimes I like their ideas so much that I add them to my own list. In case this helps you too, here are some of mine.

Over the last six years, I have written things like:

Ticked Off	Still On The List
☐ Get a cleaner ☐ Take parents on holiday with us ☐ Take 50% of summer holidays off ☐ Take all the summer holidays off ☐ Take the kids to London ☐ Take the kids to Disney ☐ Book a holiday ☐ New Chanel perfume ☐ Buy garden furniture set ☐ Bring in a home organiser ☐ Take the kids to Paris ☐ Get a puppy ☐ Gucci sunglasses ☐ Work with a personal trainer and nutritionist ☐ Get the house painted and decorated professionally ☐ Pink Macbook ☐ Large amethyst ☐ Private yacht charter ☐ New York retreat ☐ Get support with my business	☐ Buy a house at the beach ☐ Maldives water bungalow holiday ☐ Family trip to Australia ☐ Bernese mountain dog puppy ☐ First class air travel ☐ Pilates reformer machine ☐ Peloton ☐ Work 4 days a week ☐ Trip to Costa Rica ☐ Get garden extended and landscaped ☐ Travel to Borneo ☐ See the swimming pigs in Bahamas ☐ Go to Amalfi coast ☐ Pink Gucci bag ☐ Safari holiday with kids ☐ Go to Rome ☐ Take the kids to Iceland ☐ Lapland trip at Christmas ☐ Caravan or motorhome ☐ Seychelles ☐ See blue whales ☐ Trip to Antarctica to see the penguins and the long days ☐ Help both kids buy their first home

It's not enough to write your list and then forget about it. Get obsessed with checking your list and ticking things off.

If something isn't achieved one year, so long as you still want it, just moved it into the next year. My beach front home has been on the list since 2018 and one day it will be a reality.

There is nothing more empowering than seeing the things that were once beyond your reach and are now just a standard part of your life. It gives you gratitude for what you have and how far you have come, and also belief and courage that the things still to be ticked off will come, that even the big things will one day feel like small things that are easily within your reach.

That's the fun, what's in it for me, what can I be, do and have part. Why shouldn't you have the experiences and possessions you want?

But beyond your own lifestyle, there is often another driver too. This takes us to our next section.

Meaning and Purpose Two: External and Mission Driven Impact

This is the impact you want to have. It is the difference you want to make in the world. It is the way you want to help your clients and the ripple effect that may come from that, or possibly how you want to leverage your business success to make a difference in the world in some way.

You might already be super clear and focused on that. Or you might not be quite yet. Or maybe you don't want to change the world. Wherever you are on that spectrum, it is all valid.

If you are still in the place where you worry about how to pay the bills, pay off a credit card, save a deposit for your home, or feed your family, that is your absolute priority. However, once you satisfy these needs, and feel secure that this need will always be met, that's when your mind will turn to your bigger motivations, your meaning and purpose and your bigger, or external, reasons.

Your mission can change as time goes on. In my psychology student days I studied Maslow's pyramid of needs. When we satisfy our most basic needs (at the bottom of this pyramid) we can turn our attention towards more complex needs.

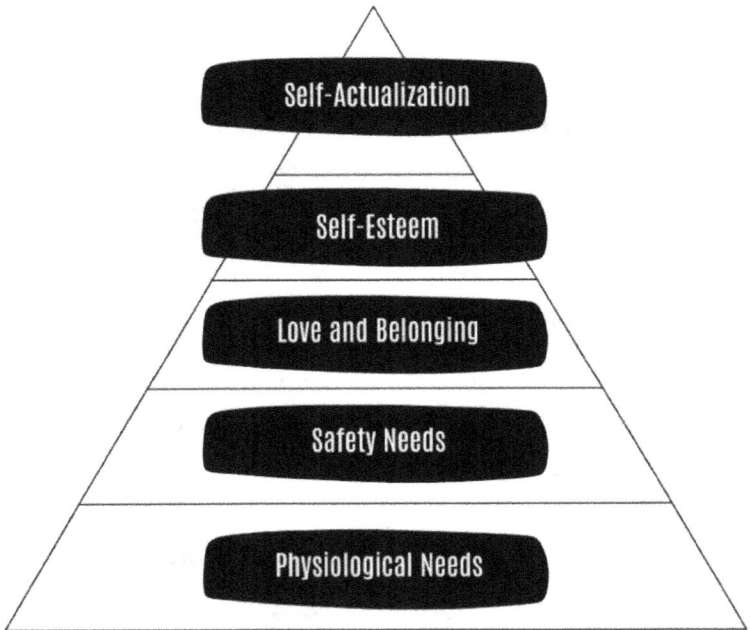

For me that bigger, broader impact driven mission looks like:

- Helping good people launch and scale good businesses that do good things in the world. I help them create a better situation for themselves and those they love, but very often their business also creates good, so there is a ripple effect.

- By helping women in business, I am helping to close the huge gender pay gap in entrepreneurship and create more wealth, independence and freedom where traditionally it has been lacking.
- I am building something for me and for my family, but beyond that, creating wealth in my business allows me to do whatever charitable or pro bono work I choose, and to make regular donations to charities I support. I have always done this in my businesses, but I only have the luxury of doing so because I am successful.

Other examples of wider external missions include that of the bank with which I hold my business account, which plants a tree for every new client, or other businesses which pay for a child's education or provide a hot meal to someone who needs one. Like Toms, with their one-for-one, giving children pairs of shoes. Like my friend Dani Wallace, with her incredible Fly Anyway Foundation, supporting survivors of domestic abuse and violence to thrive through entrepreneurship. She supports this with a percentage of the proceeds from her business.

- What change do you want to see in the world?
- What is your mission?
- How will your work improve the lives of your clients or have a ripple effect in the world?
- What does creating a consistent income for yourself allow you to do or achieve?

This can be on a big scale or a local scale.

Be super clear on why you do what you do and why you are so passionate about it so you can use that passion to drive you. Write a list of all the impactful things you can choose to do when you hit that big goal. What will you be able to do that is meaningful for you?

Who are you helping? If you do well, who else will do well? How might others benefit?

* * *

Your Goals and Purpose Will Evolve

When I first launched into solo-entrepreneurship in late 2016, I had a newborn and a two-year-old and I was coming out of postnatal depression which had hit me hard and completely out of the blue earlier that year. It was linked to my feelings about going back to work after maternity leave. I knew something had to change. Life was too short to be miserable, however well-paid I was, and I decided to do something different.

My goal was to start my own business and earn enough money in the six months before I was due back at work to be home with the kids, be flexible and present as a parent, and be there for school drop-offs and pick-ups when the time came. (I was thinking ahead!)

But I also had a mortgage and car payments and would be walking away from very good money and benefits. To make it work I needed to earn a certain amount and I had to prove I could do it within a very short time.

I had a compelling set of goals (specific money target, powerful meaning, timebound due to the end of my maternity leave) and I did it. I achieved six-figure sales inside a brand new industry in a start up in under six months.

In that first year I didn't think any wider or bigger than that. It was a completely blinkered focus on getting to that goal as I knew success was non-negotiable. When I'd achieved that goal, I got a bigger goal of having more free time, affording to do more things as a family, having all school holidays off, and then travelling more with the kids. I also started to attach more external impact to my goals. I found true motivation and satisfaction in helping others to create financial freedom and success on their terms through entrepreneurship.

My goal has grown again in terms of lifestyle. I want to travel with the kids to lots of faraway places - we are currently working our way through a travel bucket list of over thirty countries and the kids have some incredible trips they want to take. I am so inspired and motivated to do that with them.

I am also reaching and impacting more entrepreneurs than ever before and really starting to see the momentum and power of the business that I am building.

The goals will become bigger again. I want to continue to enjoy freedom and travel with my family, but I also want to create generational wealth for them. I want to reach and impact more people than ever before, and create a bigger movement. I want to change the industry and change the statistics.

At each step of the journey my personal goal and impact goal get bigger.

All this has happened in around six years. What is exciting and scary and big for me now feels incredible compared to where I was at the start when I just wanted to pay the bills and be around more for the kids.

I keep all my old notebooks and goals lists because I am motivated by a record of how quickly I can move.

My goals list from January 2017:

1) Get my first hundred customers so that I could hand in my notice by April and not return to my Director's role in recruitment after maternity leave.

My goals list from January 2019:

1) Make my first £1000 from coaching

2) Set up a paid £99 power hour and promote

3) Learn how to use Instagram

Fast Forward to 2023:

- I work with incredible clients and have been fully booked all year
- I speak on stages
- I have written this book
- I host international retreats

What an absolute dream. The version of me that wrote those goals in 2017 and in 2019 had no idea these things were going to happen or that they'd feel so big. But the goals I wrote in 2017 and 2019 felt huge, meaningful and exciting at that time too.

Because I can see how far I've come, I know how far I can still go.

* * *

Takeaways:

- Take the time to feel into your external, mission driven impact goal. How are you making the world a better place? What are you proud of? Have fun with this one.
- Be crystal clear on your lifestyle goals.
- Then combine the two. This is like rocket fuel for your motivation. You are unstoppable because your purpose isn't vague. It is the very core essence and truth of who you are and what you want to do with this one life you have. It will drive you with passion and urgency.

If your current goals don't do that, this is a clear sign to indeed take time to dream bigger and think about what you really want. It is all yours for the taking when you create more sales in your business.

* * *

Lastly: Do This Exercise. It Might Change Everything!)

Start with the big picture.

- What does success mean for you?
- Why are you doing what you do?
- If anything and everything is possible for you, what would you like to achieve?
- When you achieve that, what will you be doing in your business and your life five years from now? What does your day look like? Imagine it in as much detail as possible. How do you feel about this?

Set a timer on your phone for fifteen minutes. Remove distractions, sit down, close your eyes, and think deeply about these questions.

When time is up, make some notes. When you put pen to paper you can just let ideas flow out.

Many people think they know what they want before they do this exercise. By the time thinking time is up they realise they are building something they don't actually want. This happened to me in 2018, and the realisation changed everything. What made sense on paper and in a business plan didn't align with what I really wanted. If I hadn't tapped into that with an exercise like this one, I'd have built a business I didn't want.

We entrepreneurs are good at spotting opportunities and gaps in the market. Just because we see a gap, doesn't mean we have to be the ones to fill it, unless we really want to build that business. It might be a good idea or a good business opportunity, but it might not be the right idea or opportunity for you.

Take the time to be sure you are building a business that lights you up. And if your business doesn't make you feel like that, it is within your power to change it. Maybe change is not practical straight away, but build a transition or an exit plan and work towards it. You are in control of every step and as the CEO of your business and your life, you get to choose.

Be intentional about what you choose.

Chapter 7

Your Success Plan

"Begin with the end in mind."

— Dr Steven R. Covey, *The Seven Habits of Highly Effective People*

You should now have a huge, powerful vision that feels incredibly rich and exciting. Let's turn that into an actionable plan.

Start with the end in mind. If the end goal is a £1m turnover five years from now, work backwards to map out the steps between then and now. What would you need to be achieving in four years? In two years? This year?

Then turn this year's goals into SMART goals. (Remember those? You will if you've ever worked in corporate.)

SMART refers to goals that are:

- **Specific.** The goal should be clear and specific to focus your efforts and help you feel truly motivated to achieve it.
- **Measurable.** A measurable goal means you can track your progress. Assessing progress helps you to stay focused, meet your deadlines, and feel the excitement of getting closer to your goal.
- **Achievable.** Your goal also needs to be realistic and attainable. In other words, it should stretch your abilities but remain possible.
- **Relevant.** Make sure your goal matters to you, and that it aligns with other relevant goals. Retain control of your goals, even though we all need support and assistance to achieve our goals.
- **Time-Bound.** Every goal needs a deadline to give you a focus and something to work toward.

This approach helps you create objectives that are clear and impactful and are the easiest way to link your vision, your mission and all that is important to you in your day-to-day actions in your business. Even if you are bogged down in the mundane 'doing' you still know exactly why. Every move you make is linked to your big goals and vision and that's why you get up and do it every day, even when it is hard or you are tired.

Let's Get Planning

"A Goal without a Plan is Just a Wish."

— Antoine de Saint-Exupéry.

You need a plan to drive your business forward and get results on repeat but you might not have one. If you do, perhaps you tend to overcomplicate things. Working out how to get from A to B is simple when you break it down into smaller steps.

You should be able to answer these questions at any given time:

1. What is your revenue goal?
2. What offers are you selling?
3. At what price point?
4. Do you have capacity to deliver enough of this, at this price point, to hit your financial goal?
5. Are there gaps in your product suite? If so, how will you fill them?
6. Who are you selling them to?
7. What is the sales message?
8. How will you get your offer in front of the right people?
9. What support do you need in terms of tools, tech, team, anything else?

10. What might go wrong? How can you mitigate those risks?

11. Is every one of these answers aligned with achieving your bigger goals?

12. Does this plan feel good? Is it energising and exciting?

13. If there is resistance or bits that make you sigh, how can you make it feel better?

14. What is working well right now that you can do more of?

15. What isn't working that you can stop doing?

Take a notepad and work through these questions. Repeat as often as you need to until you are used to planning and executing that plan. I do this quarterly but track progress and results weekly and monthly.

When you have a clear vision, you can map out all the steps and then you just need to execute the plan. It's the difference between getting in your car with a clear destination in mind, somewhere you really want to be for an important reason, entering it in your sat nav and getting there easily versus meandering wherever the wind blows you and down whichever road you like the look of, or spotting a nice looking car in front of you and following it wherever it goes for a while before you see a sign you like the sound of and veering off that way, and just hoping you end up where you want to be.

You'd never, ever do that in your car, but so many hard-working people do exactly this in their business.

No more!

Action Planning

Have clear monetary goals for every year, every quarter and every month. Track these goals daily and weekly so you know exactly where you are against the plan.

This will allow you to know exactly what actions you need to take. You will know what suits your business model and your offer suite and then you know what to do to get the right number of sales in.

Example One: Someone wants to sell two £5k consultancy packages.

- To sell at that level, they probably want to do discovery calls.
- If they know they convert at fifty percent, they need to have four discovery calls booked. I'd say five or six just to be sure.
- They need to have perhaps thirty conversations inviting people to a call after their first interactions.
- Therefore they need to start conversations with one hundred potential new leads, assuming thirty percent will reengage.
- Now they need to decide their strategy to get one hundred new leads.
- They will look at what worked for them previously. This may be keynote speaking at an industry event, attending networking, posting content on social media, emailing their list, offering free value and

engaging with those who consume it, or reconnecting with previous clients. It is most likely a list of all of that.

Working backwards from the desired result, they can plan their key activities for the month.

Example Two: Someone wants to make £4000 by selling products ranging from £29-£75.

- They know the average customer spend is £40.
- They need to make one hundred sales.
- If page views convert to purchases at a rate of ten percent, they need to drive one thousand people to the sales page.
- They can figure out how to do that.
- *Or* they can set themselves a target of increasing the average spend to £60 by implementing pricing strategies like three for two, two for £60, or free postage on spend over £50.
- *Or* they can look to increase their conversion rate from ten percent to twelve percent.

In reality, they may do all these things. Because they have metrics, data and a plan, they can do it well.

Example Three: Someone has a group coaching programme at £750.

- They want twenty people on the programme, which is a sales target of £15,000.

- They can plan a free challenge or masterclass to launch it.
- Selling in this way previously converted at ten percent so they need at least two hundred attendees on the free training.
- To bring in two hundred sign-ups they need to grow their audience and nurture them, borrow from other people's audiences, email their list, promote the challenge on Facebook, and perhaps run ads to it over at least the twelve weeks prior to their challenge.

These examples are made up but if you link all your activity together you will see at what rate you convert. Then you can understand exactly which activities are key to drive performance and to get your desired results.

These activities become your daily routine. You will turn yourself into a sales machine by setting these clear KPIs, achieving or exceeding them, and seeing the results come in.

The more you do these activities, the more you convert. The better you become at these activities, the more your conversion rates increase.

The benefits are twofold. You gain momentum and traction. Instead of selling two £5k packages you sell four. You reach capacity at five of those packages a month so you raise your prices to £10k. You also create a different £2k offer that allows you to serve more people...

In the final chapter of this book, you can find some recommended KPIs and daily activities that you might want to incorporate into your business.

Operate as a CEO, even if you are a solo business owner. Know your numbers, commit to the activity, set your goals and plan your week. Block out non-negotiable time for your key activities. At the end of each week and each month, review what has gone well, what hasn't gone well, what you've learned and what you need to work on the following week.

Go to www.annapayne.online/book for more resources to help you create your vision and turn it into a strategic plan.

Chapter 8

The Sales First Approach

So many people tell me they want to sell but don't have time. Or they meant to do that all week but didn't get around to it. I get that as a business owner you are juggling many priorities. However, I also know that if you do not create time for sales, you are building risk into your business and missing out on opportunities and sales.

Make Sales a Priority!

You may be head down, delivering to clients, working in your business, and at capacity so you don't take time to build a pipeline. But what if a big client leaves you or stops buying? What if two key clients give notice in a month and you are down eighty-five percent of your income? What if you finish delivering on that sale and you have no leads or inquiries? You have built a revenue roller coaster for yourself.

Even when you are working full tilt in your business, also make time to work *on* the business, and specifically time for sales. It means your income can be far steadier and more predictable than the boom/bust where you see your income spike and crash.

I have been implementing Sales First in my own business and encouraging my clients to do so too. It is because of the Sales First process that I make sales almost every single day.

I call it 'Sales First' because as well as checking in on my sales goals and plans at least every Monday, I also have a 'sales hour' every day between nine and ten am. Sales is my first task of the week and first task of the day. This timing suits me because after my school run/dog walk commitments are fulfilled, I get home, make a coffee, catch a breath, and regardless of what else the day holds I am in my sales hour.

That time can be used for lead generation, new conversations, follow-up, or making offers, but it is time for generating and converting leads *only,* working from my leads tracker. (You can grab a copy of this by going to www.anna payne.online/book)

Use this time for nothing else. No sneaky scrolling on Instagram, no playing on Canva, no 'research', no 'faffing'... It is the time to take focused action which leads to inquiries and sales. And it works.

Whatever else the day holds, however busy your inbox gets or whatever urgent things crop up, your sales work is done so you can keep getting leads, inquiries and clients.

If you can't commit to a daily hour, what can you commit to? Thirty minutes? An hour twice a week? Try it. Block out the time in your diary and commit to it as a non-negotiable. Be consistent for a month, and I think you will be amazed by the results you create.

Will you try it? I would love to know if you like the idea of a 'Sales First' approach. If you do schedule this into your day, I'd be thrilled if you tagged me on your Instagram stories so I can cheer you on.

Chapter 9
Pricing

People can really struggle with the issue of pricing. Although this is a sales book, not a book on pricing, you will struggle to have sales conversations and get your offers out there if you are unclear on pricing.

People usually have two big questions when it comes to pricing. Both will directly impact your sales success.

Q1: How much should I charge?

Q2: Should I share my prices publicly/on my website?

Let's address these so that you are clear and confident about your pricing, meaning you are excited to show up and sell your products and services and talk directly about how much they cost.

A product is worth what customers are prepared to pay for it. There are buyers at all price points, and you should never assume what people will or won't pay.

You do not have to be the cheapest in your market: you can compete with larger rivals by offering a more personal service, value-adds or better value for money. You also need to make a profit.

Price positions you in the marketplace. It tells customers where to place you in relation to your competitors. The more you charge, the more value or quality your customers will expect for their money. This is a relative measure. If you are the most expensive provider in your market, customers will expect you to provide the best service.

Everything the customer sees must be consistent with these higher quality expectations — packaging, environment, promotional materials, website, letterheads, invoices, and so on. Existing customers are generally less sensitive about price than new customers, which is a good reason to look after them well.

Do you have very clear set prices? Do you stick to them? I speak to a lot of people who 'wing it' when it comes to pricing. That never feels good.

Let's get you clear and confident so that next time you talk to someone about your offers you can be completely upfront with a schedule of prices, instead of mumbling about how it normally costs £X but I'll only charge you £Y, giving a hefty discount for no reason, and then beating yourself up for shooting yourself in the foot yet again when it comes to money.

Do you charge enough? A lot of people undercharge and undervalue their work. Not only do they try to deliver products and services at a low cost, they also provide incredible quality and great client proximity and service.

Over-delivering whilst undercharging is a horrible combination because it can lead to burnout and overwhelm as you struggle to earn enough. It can also lead to being perceived as cheap in the marketplace. I've known several people lose bids for work because they've gone in too cheap and been told afterwards that because their price was so far below market rate, they were perceived as lower quality.

We know that's not true... but perception is reality. Charging higher prices can sometimes lead to a perception of higher value. Even with all I know about how badly entrepreneurs can undercharge, when I see things I like that are really cheap I still catch myself thinking it can't be very good.

This triangle shows the three areas any business can compete in.

- Value/Price
- Service
- Quality

Quality

Value/Price £££   Proximity To Clients

You *cannot* compete on all three points of the triangle. Pick one you want to be known for, a secondary one you can lean towards if you like, and sacrifice the third.

I see small business owners tie themselves up in knots time and time again by trying to compete on all three elements.

If you are going to compete on price and be known for low prices, you need a model which scales and involves little client proximity. Either that or you have to compromise on quality.

If you want to be known for a great client experience with high levels of quality and service, you'll charge more. This is where most small businesses should sit (although they can perhaps increase profitability or price themselves slightly lower than larger organisations with bigger overheads).

As an example, Ryanair is known for being a low-cost airline. They are famous for their terrible customer experience, low quality and lack of customer service and they parody this on their social media. But people book them because they are cheap and they mainly run to schedule. They have no illusions about what to expect.

At the other end of the spectrum is Emirates first class, or even a private jet; the most luxurious flying experience, opulent, comfortable, and inaccessibly expensive for many, but just right for the clients they want to attract.

If you want to have the best quality, the best service *and* be the cheapest, where is the give? It can only come out of your time and profits.

Look at this triangle and plot out exactly where you want to sit. It may be different for each of your offers.

For me, my client work will always be about quality.

- My one-to-one and consultancy work offer quality and service so price is a premium.
- When I drop my prices people still get quality but there is far less client proximity. You can join my brilliant value membership which is a group situation rather than a bespoke strategy for you. Or you can read this book at a really low price point but there is no proximity to help you implement it.

Plot out where you want to sit on this triangle for each of your products. Stop trying to compete on price as well as over-delivering everywhere else.

Low Prices Aren't a Sales Strategy

If you compete solely on price, you will always find someone in the market willing to undercut you. I am in some local Facebook groups and see people looking for service-based business owners but *'don't want to pay the earth'*. Let's take personal trainers. Someone posts that and I see PTs falling over themselves in the comments to show how cheap they are. It makes me sad for them.

I'll train you four times a month, I'll do a nutrition plan for you, and you have me on Whatsapp seven days a week for £70. I know people do that because they want to get more clients but at that price point how much time and attention can they really give their clients? If they want to earn a living, they will have to work with *a lot* of clients. It is not a sustainable pricing model. In fact, it is a race to the bottom to see who can offer the most for the least amount of money. In that kind of race, no one wins.

People Buy What They Want and Are Less Price Sensitive Than You Might Think

Here's a hard truth: if people don't perceive your offer as valuable at £1000, they will not perceive it as valuable at £700 or £500 or £100.

Most people will consider price but fundamentally we buy what we want. We don't buy the cheapest house we can get. We don't buy the cheapest food or go on the cheapest holidays. We don't choose our clothes or accessories based on what's the cheapest. We don't drive the cheapest cars. We don't choose the cheapest services... or employ the cheapest people.

We choose what we want and what suits our needs and wants the best.

Instead of trying to reduce the price, work on:

1. Understanding the wants and needs of your clients (their buying triggers).
2. Making your offer as valuable and attractive as possible.
3. Telling people about your offers, and asking them to buy.

Please review your prices too! Where are you underselling your value?

Money Mindset

I had never heard the term *money mindset* until around five years ago when I got into the online business world and started doing lots of work on myself. I have learned that it is important to have 'the right money mindset'. That is, the right attitudes, beliefs and confidence around money. When I first charged for my service I wondered if people would pay. I undercharged, worked for free, and felt a little embarrassed to share my prices and awkward talking about money.

I observe this in my clients, particularly women, especially clients who have come from helping and caring professions.

If you feel any shame, fear or doubt around your pricing, you need to work on it to prevent it having an impact on your sales.

* * *

The Gender Pay Gap in Entrepreneurship

Did you know there is a huge gender pay gap in entrepreneurship?

The Rose Review, formally titled "The Alison Rose Review of Female Entrepreneurship", was commissioned by the UK government and led by Alison Rose, the CEO of NatWest

Group. Published in 2019, the report highlighted the barriers faced by female entrepreneurs in the UK.

One of the significant findings from the Rose Review was the gender disparity in entrepreneurial outcomes, including earnings. The review noted that businesses run by women are, on average, only forty-four percent of the size of male-led businesses in terms of their contribution to the economy, measured in terms of turnover.

The research further showed that whilst this disparity in earnings was attributed to a perceived skills gap, that has been proven over and over to not be real.

* * *

Raising Your Prices

I often encourage entrepreneurs to raise their prices, especially if they have charged the same amount for a long time. You can do it in one go, or you may prefer to do it in gradual increments, which can make the process smoother for your business and your clients. Perhaps review and raise prices quarterly until you get to a comfortable point.

Should I Show My Prices Publicly?

Yes, is the short answer. Without doubt, sharing your prices upfront helps you to:

- Build trust.
- Get more inquiries.

- Attract more qualified leads and inquiries.

Many sales coaches suggest not sharing your prices online, so that people book a call or send an inquiry, and then you can sell them on the value and get their buy-in before you share the price.

This approach is fundamentally flawed. Firstly, you are wasting your time and someone else's time on a call when neither of you has any idea whether they can afford it.

You are also starting each potential relationship in a way which feels underhand and manipulative. Unless this is the client experience you are going for, be honest and upfront about prices. Sell on value.

By not sharing your prices you potentially miss out on many opportunities because lots of consumers will not inquire or enter into a sales process until they know the price. (I won't.) I dislike the idea of getting into an awkward conversation about an investment when I don't know how much it is going to cost me. I might like a product I see online but if I can't see a price it is unlikely that I'll send a message to ask. If someone shares a piece of art, or a dress, or a service *and a price* or even a 'starting from' price, I am much more likely to inquire or just buy.

Rightly or wrongly, people make assumptions about prices when they aren't shown. Many of us have been brought up with the belief that if a price isn't visible it means it is really expensive. There is a saying that 'if you have to ask, you can't afford it'.

People generally don't have the time or patience to mess about. If you make people work too hard to find out how much things cost, they will just move on. In this connected digital world, there are so many choices and options.

One final point on this. When I start working with a new client, they are very often undercharging. In fact, their services are a bargain so the fact they aren't shouting about their prices baffles me.

Share your prices or, if you are in an industry where it's not an exact price, share a range, a ballpark, a starting price point or some other frame of reference. People want and need to know this to build trust and move towards a buying decision. Today's consumers expect pricing transparency early in the decision-making process. With easy access to competitor pricing online, customers may view evasion on price as a red flag or a lack of transparency.

* * *

Pricing Transparency

A few years ago I earned a big bonus and wanted to buy a new car. I had seen a used car I really liked and I knew what I wanted to spend.

Me: *How much is that car?*

Sales Associate: *What's your monthly payment budget?*

Me: *I'm not sure. I'll probably pay cash or finance part of it myself so please just tell me the price.*

Sales Associate: *Well, I really need to know your monthly budget and what you can afford for a monthly payment so we can work it out for you.*

Me: *I just want to know the price. I won't be taking your finance.*

Sales Associate: *Tell me what you can afford and we'll see if we can get you into that car.*

Me: *Look, I really like that car and I probably have the means to buy it. I just need to know the price. If you can't tell me that, we are going round in circles.*

Sales Associate: *How about I go and get my manager and we sit down with you and run some numbers to see if we can get you a deal?*

Me: *Are you sure you can't just give me a price? I am leaving now!*

It was 2012 and years ago but sticks in my mind because it was one of the worst buying experiences of my life.

I went next door to a different firm and within an hour had ordered and customised a brand new BMW. It was such a smooth and simple buying process. They made me feel like a valued customer and were totally clear on the costs. They walked me through all the upsells and extras. I live in Scotland so of course I was going to pay extra for heated seats. I love music: of course I paid for the media pack. I wanted a panoramic roof so that was added on.

I had been to five garages and experienced almost nothing but rudeness, sexism, misogyny, price withholding, and disbelief that I was buying a luxury car. I was so scarred by the experience before ordering the new car that I still drive that same 2012 plate car today. It probably needs to be replaced soon, so it will be interesting to see whether car showroom sales tactics have improved in the last decade. Let's hope so.

* * *

Part 3
Your Audience

Vision: Define your goals and set targets for a clear, focused approach.

Audience: Get visible with a clear, compelling message to build your audience.

Lead Generation: Take daily action to generate and nurture leads.

Unlock sales: Make compelling offers and convert leads into sales.

Excellence: Deliver with excellence and leverage your success.

Chapter 10
Who Is Your Ideal Client?

The most successful businesses are those which are client-centric. That is, they know and understand their clients deeply. Everything they do from message to products is built on this deep understanding of their clients' wants and needs.

Start a business selling products or services you love, and then try to find an audience to buy them.

or

Know who you want to serve and sell to, build a deep under-standing of their wants and needs, then sell them exactly what they want and need.

Can you see why businesses that are client-centric rather than product-centric tend to have a far easier time when it comes to sales? This is especially true for service businesses.

Before you dive into creating offers or crafting content, the first crucial step is to understand your ideal client. When you know who you want to work with, you can design strategies to attract exactly these kinds of people.

- Who do you want to work with?
- Where are they?
- What do they need?
- What do they want?
- Do they *know* they want and need the product/service/solution/transformation you offer?
- Really importantly, are they ready and willing to invest in it? (if they don't have the awareness and/or the ability and willingness to invest, they are not ideal clients!)

Knowing who you want to buy from you, and who you are talking to in your marketing as you build an audience, is key to success in all stages of your sales and marketing.

Nail Your Niche

Too many business owners start with the wrong question. You should start by figuring out who you want to work with and then create products that this particular group desperately wants and needs, rather than asking what you want to create. It is the difference between a customer-focused business and a product-centric business. It is a deciding factor in whether you have a thriving, fully booked business or a business where it feels like an uphill struggle to sell.

When you know your audience, you can go really deep in one niche.

Let me give you an example from the viewpoint of a customer:

You love holidays and travel and Costa Rica is your dream destination. You want to book a trip there for next year. One day you're scrolling social media and you see an ad for a gorgeous hotel in Costa Rica. But you have two young kids and you aren't sure it's for you, so you have a quick look but then scroll past.

You soon see another ad for a gorgeous hotel in Costa Rica that advertises itself as a family hotel with lots of kid-focused activities and facilities as well as a luxury experience for adults. This looks more interesting. You research the hotel a little and bookmark their website/follow them on Instagram.

Your family has recently become vegan. Later that day you see a third ad. This one is for another gorgeous hotel in Costa Rica that advertises itself as a luxury family hotel with great facilities for your kids. It also talks about how being a zero-waste, sustainable hotel and the menu is fully plant-based. You instantly look up prices and availability. In your head this feels like the perfect fit.

As the vegan family of four who want to go to Costa Rica together, you will almost certainly choose the third hotel.

☐ Location

☐ Family-focused

☐ Plant-based

This is three levels deep on a niche. When you get three levels deep, you can become really clear on who you want to attract, and talk to their wants and needs in a far more compelling way. When you try to serve everyone, you usually cannot get specific enough or you only go one level deep on a niche. Two is better, but when you start to niche even further you can really clarify who you are talking to and serving.

The Exception That Proves the Rule

If your business is in a unique position but people already know they want and desperately need it, then yes you can serve everyone. Camooweal Roadhouse is a remote petrol station situated in the Australian outback, right as you leave Queensland and head into the Northern Territory towards Tennant Creek. It is the only stop for travellers crossing the border into the Northern Territory for two hundred and sixty kilometres. It is massively expensive, and you typically queue for around twenty minutes to get a pump. Everyone knows they want and need to fuel up there.

A foolish traveller who was responsible for map-reading in the passenger seat of a camper van once misread the map. Not realising that the edges of a map are repeated on the next page (this was before sat-navs and smartphones) she confidently urged the group on past the lines of camper vans and cars waiting to fuel up, saying no, it'll be fine; there's another petrol station just a few miles away. She said they didn't have to wait in those queues. Surely the next one would be quieter because everyone was stopping here. Ha. There was not another one and about One hundred kilometres in, it became very apparent that there was not another petrol station.

This was me. I was the map-reader who made this ridiculous error. Somehow we kept going and must have been running on fumes. Twenty kilometres shy of the next petrol station we glided to a halt at the side of the deserted outback road. With much ridicule and unsolicited 'helpful' advice, a convoy of Australian campers eventually helped us out and took us to the next roadhouse.

Local businesses with bricks and mortar premises may want and need to niche, but geography will also play its part.

When you are online, being super specific helps you hugely.

- Niching helps your customers feel certain that something is for them.
- Clarity and certainty lead to sales. That petrol station definitely needs a huge flashing sign to say it is the last petrol station for a long way!
- Confusion (questions such as *What is this? Who is it for? Is it right for me?*) leads to low conversions outside of your immediate circle who know, like and trust you.

When you niche, you can talk in a more compelling way, claim your area of expertise, and become known for something. You become the go-to person for that.

Even if you do lots of things and you help lots of people, when you decide on the common characteristics of who you want to help, how they self-identify, and the single most powerful way you can help them, you become one hundred percent right for a small group of people. You create content, offers and services for exactly those people instead of trying to be a jack of all trades and be thirty to fifty percent right for a larger group with varied needs. If you are a consumer who do you look to buy from? The expert, right?

Example:

I'm a mechanic and I fix and service most vehicles.

or

I'm a classic VW Camper van expert and I lovingly repair and customise VW classic campers.

If I am the proud owner of a classic VW Camper, there is a clear and obvious choice.

By niching, instead of being a bit right for most people, you become one hundred percent right for a smaller pool of people. It becomes much easier to stand out and to be selected and the right people feel compelled to work with you. You are the obvious choice.

I'm a business coach and I can help you grow your business.

or

I help ambitious, professional service providers to make more sales online in a way that feels really good for them and their clients, so they can earn more money, create more impact and enjoy freedom and success on their terms.

It's the same when I buy in support or strategy to my business. When I wanted help with my tech, I specifically went to an online business manager who owns a tech VA agency and specifically helps online coaches using Kajabi. When I wanted to scale my business through groups and programmes rather than doing more one-to-one work, I joined programmes and masterminds that focused on exactly this.

People who do really well in business coaching tend to have a niche within business, like teaching Facebook ads, or teaching small business owners how sell to corporates, or how to get into high ticket luxury sales, or how to manage their cash and investments. Consider where you are in terms of niche and whether you have scope to get even more niche. Be even more specific.

When you're not yet fully booked this might feel counterintuitive. The scarcity part of us wants all clients, any client, every client. But the minute you clarify what you do, who you help, and what you want to be known for, the easier it becomes.

This is not to exclude or alienate certain groups, but instead to help you understand the most common shared traits and tendencies so you can create content specifically tailored to the people you most want to help and that need our products or services the most.

When you do that you inspire a passionate response from those people your products and services are tailor made for, as opposed to trying to please everyone but coming across as bland, dull or passionless because of the lack of focus.

Good marketing messages should repel those clients that aren't right for you, just as much as it attracts those who are the perfect fit.

Why Understanding Your Ideal Client Is Crucial

1. **Targeted Messaging:** When you know your ideal client, you can tailor your messaging to speak directly to them, making it more relevant and impactful. You stand out to the right people and for the right reasons in this noisy world.
2. **Better Product Development:** When you understand what your clients want and need, not only can you create compelling marketing, you can develop products or services that genuinely meet their needs and desires.
3. **Elevate Customer Experience:** You can design a customer journey that resonates deeply with clients, leading to high satisfaction and loyalty.

Mapping Out Your Ideal Client

1. **Demographics and Psychographics:** Start by defining basic demographic details (age, gender, location, etc.). Things get interesting when you delve into their psychographics (their interests, values, attitudes and beliefs).

2. **Understand Their Problems AKA Pain Points:** What challenges or problems do they face that your product or service can solve?

3. **Why Are These Problematic for Them?** What is the ripple effect? For example, *I'm not making enough money in my small business and that's a problem because it is stressful, I'm working all the hours trying to create results, it's impacting my health, and I'm not spending time with my family. I'm constantly worried about how to pay my bills. I can't afford to go on holiday and I've had to cancel my gym membership. I'm not sleeping at night. It's impacting my family, my relationships and my health.*

4. **Identify Their Goals and Aspirations:** What are their ultimate goals and how does your offering help them achieve these?

5. **Why Are These Goals Important?** What is the positive ripple effect? For example, *I want to make more money in my small business so I can pay myself enough to create ease in my household, worry less, relax more and be able to work fewer hours and spend more time with my family. When I*

do that I can be really present at home, I can work on my health, and I can live the lifestyle I really want. I want to go to yoga three times a week, join that health club, book a family holiday and have enough time and money to do all the things we want to do together as a family.

6. **Speak their language:** How do they identify themselves? What language do they use to talk about their goals and aspirations?

7. **What have they tried before** to solve this problem?

8. **What beliefs** do they hold about what you do? For example, *That won't work for me because... Everyone who does that is.... This is only for...*

Map all of this out in a document or on a large sheet of blank paper. I love the A3 artist sketch pads for this.

You will know a lot of this already and you can also draw from conversations with and knowledge of your ideal clients. Consider the real people you work with. If you need to, strengthen that with market research.

*Quite often, business owners create products and services for an earlier version of themselves so they have a very clear idea of the client's wants and needs. If this is you, you have many insights to draw on.

Mastering Market Research to Understand Your Ideal Client

Market research is an important tool to unlock insights about who your ideal clients are, what they need, and how you can serve them better.

Business owners sometimes design a service they want to deliver but no one really wants or needs to buy, so despite their best efforts it is incredibly hard for them to get their business off the ground.

This is why market research matters, whether that means having formal conversations with people you believe are your ideal client or observing them where they hang out and listening closely to what they say, what they want and need.

Conduct market research at the start of every business, of course, but also each time you launch a new product or service.

How to Conduct Market Research

1. Define Your Objectives

- **Be Specific:** Clearly define what you want to learn from your market research, like demographics, buying patterns, problems, language, budget, etc.

2. Collect Your Data

- **First-hand Research:** Conduct surveys, interviews, or focus groups.
- **Observe:** Where do these people hang out? Who do they follow online? What communities are they in? What do they care about? What questions do they ask? You can glean so much information from watching and listening.
- **SEO and Keyword Analysis:** Understand what your clients are searching for online. The website https://answerthepublic.com/ is a goldmine of ideas for posts, blog posts and content.

3. Ask Questions Beyond Superficial Demographics

- **Psychographics:** Interests, values, lifestyle, and behaviour.
- **Pain Points and Needs:** What challenges do they face? What solutions do they seek?
- **Dig!** And keep digging with why, why is that important, what does that mean, why is that... and so on.

4. Market Analysis

- **Identify Competitors:** Who else serves your ideal clients?
- **Review Their Offers:** Understand what they do well and where gaps exist.

5. Apply Your Findings

- **Products:** Tailor your products or services to meet identified client needs.
- **Strategies:** Develop marketing messages that resonate deeply with your ideal clients.

Tips for Effective Market Research

- **Stay Open-minded:** Don't go in with an agenda, trying to make the findings fit what you want to do. This is about your clients, not you.
- **Engage With Your Audience:** Have real conversations with potential or current clients.
- **Regularly Update:** Consumer behaviours and beliefs change over time.

Next Steps

Understanding your ideal client through market research is not a one-time activity but an ongoing process. Every time I create a new offer I conduct market research to validate it before putting it on sale. Ask questions like: What would make this an absolute no-brainer easy yes for you? What questions would you have? What doubts or worries would you have? What else could I do to make it even better?

As your business grows and evolves, make sure you stay close to your customer. A commitment to understanding them on this deeper level ensures your business remains relevant, competitive, and the obvious choice for your customers.

Chapter 11
Getting Clear on the Right Message

Online and offline, people see upwards of ten thousand pieces of marketing a day. (A wild number, right?)

That is a huge amount of noise. We can't possibly pay attention to it all. Our brains are wired for survival and they continually, instinctively weigh up opportunities. They ask, *'what's in it for me?'*

To attract the attention of your ideal clients' brains, lead with a compelling message that spells out very clearly *what is in it for them.* Tell your prospective clients upfront how your offer/product/service can make them happier/healthier/wealthier, improve their relationships, or save them time or money or hassle in a way that stops them in their tracks.

Compelling benefits-based messaging will help you stand out, and get the right people engaged and ready to learn more about you. They are actively listening because you've told them you can help them.

If you dive into selling 'features' you become just another noise in the general melee that hits people from all angles. They aren't really engaged or interested. They aren't motivated to pay attention, because there's nothing in it for them. Their brain is conserving resources for when something useful and helpful comes along.

People will become interested in the deliverables or features of your offer, but first you must attract their attention with emotion, talking about a specific problem or solution that is deeply meaningful to them.

Your 'I Help' Statement AKA Your Verbal Business Card

What do you want to be known for? Are you clear on what you say when you introduce yourself? Do you say it in a way that sharpens the attention and focus of your ideal client? And once you have nailed it, do you introduce yourself this way every time? Or does it change all the time? Most people do not use a clear, consistent and compelling message about who they are, what they do, and why it matters to their potential clients. If that's you too, you are not alone.

Let's fix it. When you nail this part, things become a lot easier going forward and you start to be known for the one thing you want to be known for.

* * *

Your 'I Help' Framework

Create your 'I help' message to use in your communications and content and also as a vocal business card when you speak to others and introduce yourself anywhere:

- **I'm a** (insert title)
- **I help** (insert who you help)
- **To** (insert outcome, solution, transformation)
- **So they can** (insert immediate desired benefit)
- **And** (insert longer-term desired benefit)

Examples:

I'm a Personal Trainer who helps time-poor professional women in their forties to create a fitness routine that works for them, so they can get fitter, have more energy, feel better and enjoy a healthier, longer and more productive life.

As a Career Coach for under thirties, I guide young professionals through early career and life choices, helping them build confidence in themselves and make the right moves for a rewarding future.

I run an eco-friendly gift shop, helping the environmentally conscious find unique, sustainable gifts so they can celebrate special moments and protect our planet.

I'm a Contemporary Artist, creating large pieces of installation art that speak to modern enthusiasts. My colourful work adds a fun, vibrant touch to hotels, restaurants and public spaces, creating a beautiful, stylish and unique setting and ensuring people remember their visit.

I build e-commerce websites to help small retailers expand online with user-friendly sites, boosting their reach and digital growth so they can scale with ease.

What's your vocal business card?

* * *

Simplicity

Your message needs to be super simple. If you talked about what you do to an eight-year-old, could they grasp it? If the answer is no, you need to simplify your message. This is not because people are stupid but because they are overloaded with information from the minute they wake up and look at their phones or switch on the radio, until the minute they go to sleep. When something is complicated, unless there's already a clear reward, they won't try to work it out. They will move on to something easier.

Potential clients have no reason to be interested or invested in you *yet*. Your potential client pays attention to what will make their life happier, healthier, wealthier, better and easier.

Apply The Starbucks Test

I work a lot in Starbucks when I need a break from my home office, so I hear a lot of conversations going on around me. Very rarely do I hear people say to their friends, *'If only I could get myself unstuck and step into my power.'* Or, *'I tell you what I really need... a series of eight coaching sessions* with voxer access.' Or 'I want to find my true self and get clarity.'

Of course they don't. They talk in real terms about their current challenges, frustrations and desired outcomes. If you want to attract their attention, you should too.

If your ideal client met a friend or peer for coffee and grumbled about where they were feeling stuck or what they wanted to achieve, what would they say? What language would they use?

Speak Their Language: Use words and tones that resonate with your audience.

Highlight Relatable Scenarios: Use stories in your communication that your ideal client can relate to. Stories are way more powerful and persuasive than facts.

Storytelling in Marketing

We are hardwired to pay attention to stories. Storytelling goes back to those caveman days when early humans would tell stories around the fire, or draw stories on the walls of their caves. Stories help us to listen, understand and remember. They make us feel something. The best stories open up loops in our heads which we want to close by hearing the end of the story.

They also have the power to influence action and decision-making by tapping into psychological and emotional triggers. All of this makes storytelling the *most* powerful tool in marketing. You can make that work for your business.

We each have a unique perspective on why we do what we do. The better you are at sharing your story, the more people will be interested. Over (a short) time your stories can convert a passive audience into loyal fans of you and your brand, and then into customers. Stories will accelerate your building of knowledge and trust.

We must also understand our customers' stories and how the two intersect. When we learn to articulate this connection between what we do and what our customers truly want and need, clearly, and consistently, we have a compelling message that will connect us with our people. We become a brand that counts.

When you use storytelling well in your brand, customers do not just buy a product. They also buy into an ethos, a set of values, an aspiration; they become part of your story, movement, or community that stands for something. When you do this, you don't have to push, persuade or 'sell'. By telling your story clearly, consistently, and authentically you warm up your audience and turn them into connected, loyal fans, engaged and ready to buy from you.

What do you stand for? What will you be known for? What is your story? What stories will you tell about your clients? How does that connect with your potential clients?

Please note: While this is a story, it is not a work of fiction. The best stories are completely genuine. Don't fake it till you make it or show up as who you think you 'should' be, or how everyone else in your industry is. Be your authentic self, be vulnerable and be real. Be weird, be different, be quirky... be yourself. Your people will find you and they will love you for it.

Claim Your Expert Status

So... you will say how you help your clients, and why that matters. As well as that, you must claim your expert status, your brilliance.

This can feel hard to do (back to the good old mindset work) but if you don't believe you are brilliant at what you do, why would anyone buy it?

I am an expert at making sales and teaching others how to make a lot more sales in a way that feels really good for them and their clients.

But it took me forever to come out and say that. I came across all shy and humble when I first came online. I wanted to *show* people how good I was, not tell them. But that's not enough when you are growing a business. You have to claim your brilliance and tell people on repeat what you do that you are really good at. When you do this, you'll find a big shift; people pay attention, they understand why they need you. Because you are confident in your abilities, they feel more confident in your abilities.

* * *

Question

What are you an expert at? What is your zone of genius or your superpower? Do you claim your brilliance? Do you tell the world you are an expert? If not, why not? Go out there immediately and tell people what your secret superpower is.

* * *

And What Else?

If you are a personal brand, you should also include other components, often called secondary messaging. This is the more human part; who you are, what you care about, your values, what you do in your spare time, what matters to you, what you love, what you struggle with. Think of it as showing up as your very human, perfectly imperfect self.

I have a lovely client with the funniest, warmest and wittiest personality. She jokes that when she meets new people she keeps saying in her head, *'Don't be weird, Emma, don't be weird.'* But I think the opposite. Her personality is exactly what makes her memorable, compelling and easy to buy from. So be weird. Be you. Be more you!

Choose three things about you that you love and that are representative of who you are and how you show up, then dial into them and make them a core part of your messaging.

You don't have to share everything. Share the parts you are comfortable sharing and don't share the rest.

Look at author and money mentor Denise Duffield Thomas. She shares a lot and everyone thinks they know her, but when you add up what you know about her, the same three or four things come up over and over again. She mainly shares that she's lazy, she likes to work in situations where she doesn't have to wear a bra, she talks about her life as an ADHD entrepreneur, and she loves the beach.

Amy Porterfield styles herself as the nice girl next door. She speaks about the four-day week and easy living; she is the systems gal who breaks everything down into easy to follow steps. She has a billion-dollar business, but her messaging is all very nice girl next door.

Jenna Kutcher, photographer and Instagram influencer turned online coach, shares about body confidence, her young family and her home. She shares that she podcasts from a cupboard at home, and loves mac and cheese and yoga pants. She has a relatable persona, borne from sharing the same key facts on repeat.

These are examples of high-profile people in the online business world who share snippets of themselves on repeat. By doing so, they really connect and resonate with the people who are their people. They develop an online persona. Their audience feels like they know them well and they trust them.

You can do this too. Take who you are as a person and distil that to a few key points, then dial it up so this becomes your persona. We are all multi-faceted human beings with many, many complex thoughts, beliefs, interests and experiences. You don't have to share everything, just *enough*. Share those parts consistently. Over time people will know, like and trust you.

Make it an authentic expression of who you are. Nothing makes me happier than when I meet people in real life and they say I am exactly how I appear online. This feels like a big compliment because I know I show up as myself. To me there is nothing more disappointing than meeting someone who comes across as compassionate, warm, friendly and supportive online but in real life they are stand-offish, cold and uninterested. That has happened a few times over the years.

I share that I love to travel and work remotely because it is so important to me, but I know it also resonates with many entrepreneurs driven by lifestyle. I share my love of the beach because it is easy to; I spend a lot of time there. I share about my family because they are everything to me, and I know that resonates with many others who are building a business around family life. I talk about being an introvert, about integrity and about being nice. These are all fundamental to how I show up and how I do business.

I also talk about feminism, equity, social justice and empowering girls and women because I care deeply about these things. But if I shared about art and literature or jigsaw puzzles or fly fishing or sustainable transport, or doing cook-alongs or product reviews, it would start to get a bit noisy and confusing. So share some of you, the parts you know will resonate with your people. In case you are wondering, I love art and literature but I don't know much about it other than what I enjoy; I know nothing about fly-fishing and I can't cook!

This complete picture is the bit that makes people like you, trust you and potentially choose you over anyone else doing a similar thing to you.

For example, I love working with women entrepreneurs who are building a business around their family, who want to do huge, amazing things in the world and who also want to travel and have adventures. My messaging attracts these people.

1. First of all people buy what they want.
2. They buy a solution to a problem.
3. They buy from emotion so they buy from people they like and trust, people that resonate with them and people who inspire them because they feel they are similar or they want what that person has.

What parts of you do you feel comfortable sharing? Where are you holding back? Who are you really as a person? Don't go down the road of saying no one is interested in you so why would you post about yourself. I can post ten amazing, value-filled posts telling people exactly how to make sales. Or I can post a personal one that shares an outfit for a wedding, or our beach bonfire and the engagement will be ten times what it was on the other posts put together.

Last Point

How do you want your audience to feel when they hear your message and see you or engage with your content? There is a beautiful Maya Angelou quote which says,

> *"People will forget what you said, people will forget what you did, but people will never forget how you made them feel."*

How do you want your audience to feel? This is important at all times. You don't get a second chance at a first impression, but also because the way your audience feels needs to be consistent. Consider this at every touch point and in each customer interaction. Be aware that their interaction may not be with you in person; it might be with your Instagram account, your blogs or your YouTube videos. Are all of these doing the job you want them to do?

Make your customers feel good and they'll be loyal to you forever.

More on Selling Benefits Versus Features

(Because most people really struggle with this!)

The most common mistake when it comes to messaging is focusing too much on the features of a product or service, rather than the benefits. Understanding the difference between them and communicating accordingly will dramatically improve your results.

Features Are About Your Product: the factual statements about what your product is and does – specifications, ingredients, deliverables, times, dates, quantities, modalities, methodology, etc.

Benefits Are About Your Client: answers to the client's most important question – *'What's in it for me?'* Benefits explain how your product improves their life or solves their problems and makes them happier, healthier, wealthier or improves their life in some meaningful way. You might introduce a feature but say s*o you can (insert benefit)* or *which means (insert benefit).*

* * *

Imagine you go to a travel agent to book a dream holiday, somewhere warm and tropical where you can relax by the beach.

Agent One: I know just the place. You can fly direct from your local airport. Then when you arrive, the hotel is incredible. It's a modern, ultra luxurious five-star resort, right on the beach in the Seychelles. The suites are ocean-front and you can watch the sunrise from your private terrace. The sand is like talcum powder and it's a glorious spot for swimming, snorkelling and water sports. There's an incredible seafood restaurant on the beach and live music a few times a week. You can do some trips to other parts of the island, or if you just want to relax, the beach has little cabanas, and there is an award-winning spa on-site. It's a very relaxed, low-key, but luxurious vibe and I think you'll love it – does that sound good?

Agent Two: Great, you want to book a holiday. I have a place in mind. Included in the price are your flight and your transfers. When you get to the airport, you'll check in your bags as the airline will take your bags for you. Your flight is included; it's nine hours thirty-five minutes. On the plane you'll be served drinks and two meals and you will have a TV screen to watch a selection of films. You'll get a warm baby wipe after dinner to freshen up. Once you arrive at the Seychelles airport you'll collect your bags and clear passport control and we will have a minibus ready to take you to the accommodation. There will be water and soft drinks in the mini-bus... it will take around ninety minutes to drive to the hotel and when you get there a porter will carry your luggage to your room.

If I spoke to agent one, I'd be saying, *'Take my money.'* In fact, when I was writing the words, I was wondering whether this place exists. Can we go? If I spoke to agent two, I would be losing the will to continue the conversation. I would end the call or leave the shop. Just skip to the good parts, please! Give me the boring but necessary details if I have questions, otherwise, only once I am invested and have bought in.

* * *

Why Focus on Benefits?

- **Emotional Connection:** People buy based on emotions and then justify it with logic. Benefits speak to emotions and desires.
- **Easier Decision Making:** Benefits simplify the decision-making process by clearly showing the value proposition.

- **Stand out in the Market:** Many others who do what you do might offer similar features, but the way you frame the benefits is an opportunity to set your offer apart.

Common Mistakes

- **Listing Features Only:** A list of features doesn't tell a client why they should care.
- **Assuming Understanding:** Never assume the client will automatically understand the benefits from the features. Break them down super simply and spell it out. Every single time you list a feature add a *'so you can (insert benefit)'* 'So you can' is a really good addition to your sales copy!

How to Sell Benefits

- **Identify Key Features:** Start with what your product or service does.
- **Ask 'So What?':** For each feature, ask, 'So what does this mean for the client?'
- **Translate into Benefits:** Turn the answer into a compelling benefit statement.

Example

- **Feature:** Our business banking app uses advanced encryption.

- **Benefit:** Enjoy peace of mind knowing you are always protected by our advanced encryption.

Tips for Effective Benefit Selling

- **Use Client Language:** Talk about benefits using words and phrases your clients use.
- **Tell a Story:** Use storytelling to make the benefits more relatable and memorable.
- **Focus on Top Benefits:** Highlight the most compelling benefits that address major client needs or pain points.

Chapter 12
Getting Visible

The next step, now you know who you are talking to and how to attract their attention, is to show up consistently with that message, talking about how you (the expert, go-to person, obvious choice in your industry) can help people. All the time!

Not being visible enough to your potential clients can be one of the main blockers to sales. After all, how can people buy from you if they don't know or remember that you exist? (Or how you can help them!)

It is critical that you are:

1. Consistently visible to the right people.
2. Being visible strategically, with the right message.
3. Building trust, to engage your audience and drive more leads and inquiries.

> **This means you start to be known as the go-to person in your industry and become the obvious choice for people who want whatever it is that you offer.**

I have always been good at what I do, but when I clarified, simplified and nailed my message, that's when my business trajectory changed. I became very well known specifically for sales. I started to be recommended and to be approached with lots of opportunities. I was invited to speak at events and on stages. I was constantly tagged in social media posts looking for help with sales.

Before, when my message was about more generic business growth, business strategy, and helping entrepreneurs, I attracted some people for some things, but I was working really hard. It was all based on personal relationships, networking, and referrals. If you didn't already know me or know of me, I wasn't the obvious choice or the go-to person.

Now, I am... because I've worked hard to get here. My messaging created that for me and it can for you too when you get it right.

So, you know what to do on your messaging. Now, let's work on your visibility strategy. You need to get that good strategic, attention-grabbing and compelling message in front of your ideal clients, both in your existing audience and new people.

A word of caution. Never underestimate **how many times you should talk about what you do and how you can help people.** It is not a case of one and done. On the contrary, this is a daily task.

I have been connected to some people for years purely through business on social media and despite seeing their content regularly, and even meeting some of them in real life, I still have *no idea* what they do or whether they could help me or my clients. But I know lots of other (irrelevant) trivia about them.

This wasted effort makes me sad. Please do not be this person. **Talk daily about how you can help people.**

* * *

Action: Go and test it now. Post on your social channels, *'I'm interested to know, who knows what I do and how I help people? Comment what you think I do and let's see if I am good at sharing it with you.'*

* * *

Be Focused

There are many ways to get visible, but the worst thing you can do is try to do them all at once; that is a route to overwhelm. Do a few things, but do them consistently and to a high standard.

Choose audience building activities that make you feel happy and energised when you think of them. They should feel fun and natural for you. For some people that might be speaking at events or on a stage; for others that is doing something way less high profile. Make the best use of your strengths and create as much flow and ease as possible in your business. Remember the science earlier in this book. When you work with your natural attributes and talents you get so much more done and to a much higher level than when you force yourself to do something that doesn't come naturally. You are also much more likely to actually do it!

The best approach is to have core, tried and tested ways of being visible and then lean further into what works for you, as well as testing and trialling new ways of getting visible that you can layer on top of your core strategies.

It all takes time, and you don't have to be in all these places at once. Start with the most obvious places and then layer up from there. Keep trialling, testing and growing as you go.

Visibility when I started online looked like:

- Social media (Facebook)
- In-person networking.

Visibility now looks like:

- Social media (Facebook, Instagram and LinkedIn)
- Being an associate coach or guest expert in two other relevant groups

- Doing guest trainings in lots of memberships, masterminds and groups
- Speaking at events and conferences
- This book
- Guesting on podcasts
- Paid advertising and promotion in relevant online communities
- Collaborations

Visibility in the future will look like:

All of the above PLUS

- My own podcast launches in 2024 (so look out for that)
- Press and PR
- Awards
- Tik-Tok (maybe)
- Pinterest
- YouTube (repurposing videos and audio content)
- Paid ads on Facebook and Google
- Sponsorship of events

More Tips for Visibility Success

This might feel like a huge amount of work, but I recommend a few hacks.

1. First of all, batch and schedule. It is now possible for me to do a month's worth of content in not much more than an hour.

2. Secondly, and this is huge, repurpose and recycle content so you get as many eyes as possible on your content, and as much bang for your buck as possible when you have put work into creating something.

3. You don't always have to build from scratch; sometimes you can borrow other people's audiences and get in front of them to promote your offers. Not only are you getting a lot of eyes on you, this also presents you as a partner of someone those people already know, like and trust so they are far warmer and more receptive to you than a cold audience.

4. Consistency is key. Whatever you do, be consistent. If you decide to do a daily or weekly livestream or Q&A session on your social media, do it at the same time or day each week so people start to expect it. Send your weekly email on the same day and make it valuable every time. How can *you* get more consistent each day or week?

5. Give value. Provide your ideal client with consistently high quality, valuable content that reflects who you are and what you do. This makes people see you as a credible expert and authority, and someone they want to buy from.

6. Wherever you show up, repurpose and recycle content to get as many eyes as possible on it.

7. Mindset plays a big part in how comfortable you feel getting visible. Commit to the necessary mindset work to build your confidence and self-belief. When you feel yourself wondering *'who's interested in what I have to say anyway?'* or worrying about *'looking silly'* or feeling like an imposter who isn't qualified

or ready, go back and do the mindset work to counter these limiting beliefs and replace them with new, helpful beliefs.

Final Words: Measure and evaluate everything you do so you know your efforts are channelled in the right places. Use the data and metrics to refine as you go.

Action:

Explore new ways to get visible. Check out this list of ideas and see what jumps out at you.

1. Talk about what you do, why it matters and your passion for it. I have found clients through casual conversations everywhere from chats with ex-colleagues to nights out and even on the school run! I have also had referrals made by my hairdresser. She tells her other clients about me if they run their own business. Even my vet has proved to be a source of referrals.

2. Instagram is my favourite social media platform. Use the engagement features in stories and actively seek and connect (authentically, no spammy cold DMs) with new people to build your network and keep relationships warm.

3. LinkedIn is a great platform if you sell to professionals. Update your bio with what you do. Actively engage with new people who fit your potential ideal client profile.

4. Update your personal Facebook profile with business contact details, job title and a branded graphic as your header. Post regular content that relates to your business and connect with people in your network.

5. Build your own community on Facebook or some other platform. Offer free value and grow the community.

6. Run free or low-cost events in real life or online: from networking to a running club; wild swimming to coffee chats over Zoom; workshops, masterclasses, and Q&As. Events are a brilliant way to get known for something, be seen and build community.

7. Join and be a helpful, valuable participant in Facebook communities relevant to what you do. Many will let you advertise what you do. You can also use the group search function to find and answer questions that relate to what you do.

8. Create a 'lead magnet', a free PDF/ebook or video that people can watch in return for their email address. Share this link frequently.

9. Use email marketing. Build your email list with a freebie lead magnet and then nurture them with a weekly email to keep you relevant and front of mind.

10. Start a podcast. This is so easy to DIY and a brilliant way to reach new people and share your message as well as boost your authority in your sector.

11. If you're not ready to be a podcast host, pitch yourself as a podcast guest to shows with a relevant audience and get in front of new people that way.

12. Collaborate with other business owners to share audiences or create events or packages that add real value. For example, what else are your clients interested in? Who do you know that offers something aligned with what you do? For example, a nutritionist and a PT can easily collaborate; a brand photographer may want to collaborate with a web designer or a brand designer.

13. TikTok is the fastest growing social platform and people are having great success here - and you don't have to do dance trends either. Provide valuable content that fits your brand.

14. Use Pinterest to drive traffic to your website or email list.

15. Get featured in the press. Work with a PR professional or learn the basics yourself and make direct approaches to relevant press. There are also brilliant groups and threads on social media connecting journalists with entrepreneurs looking for press.

16. Write a book. You can self-publish easily these days and being an author with a useful book in your area of expertise gives you instant credibility. It is something fab to talk about as well as a brilliant way for people to get to know who you are and what you are all about.

17. Attend networking groups. There are many online and real-life events. Find one that suits your vibe and where your kind of client is likely to be. Don't network with the sole focus of making a sale, go in there open to collaboration and with a view to

offering support. Many brilliant things have happened to me as a result of chance meetings at networking.

18. Ask your clients to refer people to you. Consider having affiliate payments or rewards to encourage people to actively promote you and get paid for it.

19. Exhibit at festivals or attend pop up events that are relevant to your industry.

20. Add your business details, contact details, images and reviews on Google: it's free.

21. Leverage the power of video. It can build trust in what you do and connect more meaningfully with people. You can do regular livestreams or even start a YouTube channel.

22. Create content for your social channels based on your clients: client spotlights, client transformations, client wins. They are likely to repost and share, meaning lots of new eyes on what you do and a nice bit of social proof.

23. Enter industry awards.

24. Write a blog and use SEO to get it found.

25. Do an interview series over a period of weeks where you chat to lots of different people about a certain topic or theme.

Chapter 13

Social Media But For Goodness Sake, Make It Strategic

In the early days of my sales career very few people had email. No one had a mobile phone and social media hadn't even been invented. It was all about phone, face to face or, when you were in a rush to share something, the fax machine. (Remember those?)

* * *

The Fax Machine Story!

Writing that opener has put me in mind of a funny story. Although it ages me, it is a great demonstration of under-hand sales tactics.

In my first ever recruitment job we used to supply temp office staff. It was a fastest fingers first kind of business. Whoever got the right candidate's details submitted most quickly got the booking. They would often be worth hundreds or even thousands of pounds so it was high stakes.

When a client put out a requirement, it was sometimes just to us, but it was sometimes to three or four agencies at once. We had to fax candidate CVs and details through to get them booked in. One of our competitor agencies had a brilliant but awful scheme to always get the booking... they bought a second fax specifically so they could jam our fax with a two-hundred-page nonsense document, meaning we couldn't fax out while it was incoming. Our line was engaged. They faxed over the candidate details on their other number and got the booking.

Smart, but let's agree it is not a bad thing we don't use fax machines to make sales anymore... and also that this kind of underhand tactic is not the right way to achieve sales success!

* * *

I have done it the hard way. I know that social media is a gift for entrepreneurs. It is a huge opportunity to interact, to learn, to engage, to build community, to build trust and authority, and yes, to convert followers to fans and paying clients.

The ease with which we can share ideas and messages, attract prospective clients and collaborators, build community and find opportunities is staggering. It has given so many small businesses the opportunity to start and to thrive.

However, our biggest strengths can, unchecked, be our greatest weaknesses. People struggle with how much time they spend on social media. It is a full-time job for them, but because it is not being used strategically to drive conversions, this investment of resources does not achieve results representative of the time and effort invested.

I host co-working or implementation sessions, and I ask people what they are working on at that time. about the answer is often social media, planning, and content creation. An inordinate amount of people's time can go into this, for frankly very average results.

This is because their posts don't help them sell more or get the word out effectively. Or because they have created large free groups that take a lot of time but aren't being used to drive sales. It is a lot of creation and information, without really talking to their customers or making sales from it.

Get strategic so you can cut down the time you spend and multiply the results you get. Let's make a plan.

- What result do you want to achieve?
- Who are you talking to?
- What are your most engaging posts?
- What opportunities do you have to start conversations?

What is the goal?

Your time and energy are precious resources so use them accordingly. Be ruthless with your resources and continually assess, *does this task take me closer to my goals?*

The main goal is to make sure everything you do on social media helps build relationships with customers and potential customers, and to drive sales.

A good rule of thumb when it comes to social media for your business is to remember the three Cs of social media.

Content → Conversations → Conversions

Many people get stuck in content creation mode but never start conversations or convert followers to clients. Let's get clear on each step and how you can split your time more equally to do the important income generating tasks a little more.

Content: By providing engaging, relevant, and valuable information you attract and engage a specific audience. Content can help you can build trust and establish yourself as a thought leader and the obvious go-to person in your field.

Conversation: Do not just pump out more and more content. Social media is inherently social, and conversation is a two-way communication between you and your audience. Listen, engage in dialogue, respond to comments, participate in discussions, and be clear that you can have great conversations in DMs too, as it is so natural to make sales here. *However, avoid cold messaging on social media.

Conversion: Conversion is the ultimate goal of most social media strategies, where your audience takes a desired action. This could be making a purchase, signing up for your email list, downloading your app, booking a discovery call, or any other action that is valuable to your goals. The idea is to move followers along the customer journey from awareness and interest to decision and action.

Note: The three Cs are a convenient shorthand for remembering key components of a social media strategy, but there are some other important cs to consider too — elements like community building, connection, collaboration, and consistency are also important.

* * *

You have all this smart content; let's also be smart about getting maximum return on your efforts...

The biggest time drain is creating at volume so repurpose and recycle your content.

Here is how to get the most out of one piece of content:

- Record a podcast, a webinar or social media live and share it as normal.
- Post it on YouTube.
- Send an email linking to your original piece of content.
- Turn the transcript into a blog post, a LinkedIn article, and an email.
- Consider whether it is substantial enough that you can repurpose it as a PDF, a mini ebook, a lead magnet or a paid training.

- Edit it into a long copy post for your social media.
- Share snippets as an audiogram.
- Comb through the transcript for the golden nuggets and turn these into quotes to use as graphics or short snappy posts.
- Represent the key ideas in graphics.
- Create and schedule these pieces of content over the next quarter.
- Keep them. In three or six months you might want to reuse them, or perhaps tweak them… change the headline, change the graphic and repeat.
- Repeat!

From one longer piece of content, you can create multiple pieces of content… I'd say at least thirty. This represents endless opportunities to reach many people, in different ways, catering to different platforms and different content consumption preferences.

Scheduling these repurposed content pieces over the next thirty to ninety days will reinforce your message, boost your visibility and build your trust and credibility.

This is a much smarter use of your time and energy. You can also outsource it to a professional, engaging a Virtual Assistant or Social Media manager to support you. Some entrepreneurs use a golden nugget miner (best job title ever) to go through their lives and podcasts and pull out the golden nuggets for repurposing.

* * *

Use Video to Accelerate Building Trust

I strongly suggest using video on your social media, not only because it is prioritised by the algorithm of many platforms but because your viewers can really get to know you, see what you stand for, what you care about, how you talk and engage and what it might be like to work with you.

Letting someone hear your voice and how you talk is huge in terms of building the all-important know, like and trust factor that is required to make sales.

So while Instagram reels that show you lip-synching to an audio or use silent footage of you working against a background of music can be fun to use occasionally, it is the videos in which people hear your voice and see how you engage that move the dial in terms of building trust.

Get the Balance

I use a brilliant social media creation company (cluecontent.com, go and check them out!) to help me produce professional, slick, on brand video content. It tells the story of my business and lets people who are new to my world see what I look like, how I speak, exactly what I am all about, what working with me might be like, and to understand my ethos, values, approach and take on my industry. I am building a bank of watchable content people can consume as it is released or in one go when they find my account to help them move closer to a buying decision.

We create three months of content in two days. But social media is an opportunity to connect, create conversations, get your message out and create opportunities quickly, so I use a multi-layered approach and top up the professionally produced content with much more ad-hoc content. It is not slick or polished but shows behind the scenes or gives an update on what is happening in life and business. This content gets engagement that is just as good if not better, so don't wait until the conditions are perfect, your hair is done, your makeup is on, you have the perfect lighting and backdrop or whatever else you are worried about. People relate to reality and authenticity more than they do to perfection.

I also share opinion/thought leader posts which are more like mini blogs. I give my views, opinions or takes on whatever is going on in the industry right now, if it's something I want to comment on.

Review Your Performance

What type of content is working? What do people engage with most? What drives the most action in terms of engagement or leads and inquiries? Review your social media statistics in terms of reach, engagement and follower numbers and track your progress week to week and month to month so you can fix any problem areas and lean further into what is working. Notice what works for you and then do more of it!

Which Platforms?

To choose where you want to be, you need to know where your clients are most likely to spend their time online? Wherever your clients are, be there.

If you are business to business, I suggest LinkedIn. If you are business to consumer, are your people on Facebook? Instagram? Tik-Tok? What communities and groups are they part of? What creators do they follow?

I suggest focusing on one main platform and getting really consistent there. Then you can add a second platform, or a third.

My main platform at the moment is Instagram. The content I post on there crossposts onto my business Facebook page. I also post more ad-hoc content on my personal Facebook account. The same content is sometimes just straight posted on LinkedIn or occasionally different content is created depending on business objectives.

Some people will tell you to have a different content strategy for each platform. To a certain extent that may be true, but most small businesses do not have time or resources to create three different sets of content, and the potential extra reward isn't worth the extra effort required. Be pragmatic and efficient and use the work you have already done.

If there are platforms that you don't utilise, instead of ignoring them altogether I suggest you still fly a flag there without being a regular attendee. You are unlikely to drive new traffic but if someone searches for your business, they'll find it and know the next steps.

Create a profile using your title, your branded profile photo and your bio. Either create a pinned post or note in your bio/about section that you don't spend much time on this platform but if people would like to connect with you/find out more they can... X, Y, Z (insert relevant calls to action directing people to your website, lead magnets, contact form, etc.).

If you want to make it even better, include some reviews or testimonials and ways to work with you. Done. You know you won't miss out on anyone actively searching for your business, you may pick up the odd extra due to keywords in your profile, and if/when you have capacity to experiment with attracting new leads via this platform, you are set up and ready to go.

Optimising Your Social Media Profiles for Sales

When someone first hears about you, meets you, or you are recommended to them, they will typically go straight to social media to check you out. What they see determines whether they...

- engage and take a step closer to becoming your customer, *or*
- scroll away and on to the next company that is set up better than you on social media.

Optimise your social media so that when people see it for the first time it is clear, compelling and attracts people into your world. Visit your social media profiles regularly. View them through your potential client's eyes and ask yourself these questions:

- Is this compelling?
- Is my messaging immediately clear? (What I do, who it's for and why it matters?)
- Is it clear what someone interested should do next? (Apply now/book now/buy now/click here/send an email.)
- Would *I* want to buy from me/this business?
- Is there a feeling of trust, quality and professionalism (or whatever is important to your brand)?
- Can I see the key details? (Location, contact details, pricing or whatever is most important.)
- How does this account and first impression compare with others in my market?
- How much content is available to consume now to help me make a buying decision? (Links, videos, articles, reviews, ways to work with me, product lists.)
- Do I feel proud and excited to share this social media profile with potential clients, knowing it is showing the very best of my business?

Take time to review your social media through the lens of these questions.

Do a Monthly Check and Tidy Up

Visit your social media profiles regularly to review the above and do a quick health check while you are there.

- Use the same branding and brand photos across platforms for recognisability.
- Be consistency in your business name and description (unless you intentionally use different platforms to attract different types of client).
- Make sure your links are up to date and not broken.
- Are your contact and location details accessible (if relevant)?
- Is there a clear call to action?

Last Point

Remember, you do not own your social media account. Some business owners are hacked, or have their accounts suspended or shut down. Even if that doesn't happen, you are still at the mercy of the algorithm which determines who will see your posts, and when. See social media as a place for people to find you, a great place to start conversations and build trust, but as only a first step, the top of your funnel. Always work to move customers to the next stage of your customer journey, for which I recommend email marketing. You own that list, you have a note of those emails, and you get to be very specific about what you send and when.

Part 4
Lead Generation

Vision: Define your goals and set targets for a clear, focused approach.

Audience: Get visible with a clear, compelling message to build your audience.

Lead Generation: Take daily action to generate and nurture leads.

Unlock sales: Make compelling offers and convert leads into sales.

Excellence: Deliver with excellence and leverage your success.

Chapter 14
Let's Find Some Leads

You are building your audience with great messaging, strategic social media *and* a plan to consistently get visible in front of new people (the right kind of people, people who fit your ideal client profile).

You are nurturing that audience, engaging with them, and building trust. Work actively with that audience to generate **leads.** Leads are potential customers who either overtly or more subtly give us a sign that they are interested in buying from us.

The online world is noisy, each business vying for the attention of potential customers. We all show up online, but why does it feel like such a hard slog for some of us, making all the content for no results, while others make sales every time they post?

How do you stand out and attract the right audience amongst all this noise? The answer lies in lead generation and the ability to pick up those leads and convert them into sales.

I am going to challenge you to find one hundred leads. Unless you are brand new to business, I can almost guarantee that the majority, if not all, are already somewhere in your ecosystem. Leads are everywhere! Business owners need to be better at finding them, which means picking up on buying signals (even subtle ones) and taking appropriate action. When you identify who your leads are, you can follow up with them and convert them from leads to sales.

How Do You Define a Lead?

A lead is a potential client who has somehow, either overtly or more subtly, indicated some level of interest in the product or service you offer. This could be someone who has filled out a form on your website, subscribed to your email list, downloaded your freebie, attended a free training, met you at an event or networking and expressed interest, booked a call or even is consistently engaging with your content on social media.

A lead is a potential opportunity for a sale. It represents someone who has raised their hand (digitally or physically, and overtly or very subtly) to show they are potentially interested in what you have to offer. Your task is to identify then nurture these leads into becoming loyal customers.

Not All Leads Are Equal

Some leads are red hot and should be easy to turn into a sale - that person in your inbox saying they must work with you/buy from you, asking for your prices and availability or how they can buy your product.

Other leads show subtler signs of low-level interest; definitely interested but not yet ready to convert.

The difference between a business being very successful at sales or not is partly determined by the ability to recognise and respond to those subtle leads. When you capture and convert these, that's when you really start to double, treble, even 10x your conversion rate. Exciting times!

My sales process always starts with the quick wins and low hanging fruit. These are the warmest leads, so first I work on connecting with these, making offers, following up and closing the sale.

But don't stop there. Spend time at least weekly looking for those more subtle signs of interest. Note them down and commit to nurturing as many of these as possible through to the point where they are a red hot lead and then a committed buyer.

Your sales work should always be two-pronged:

- Find the quick wins and the easy sales.
- Work on the prospects who are interested but not yet ready to buy (but might soon be).

How you engage with and follow up with a lead will be nuanced, depending on whereabouts they are in the buying journey.

The table below shows a range of leads, some already with a very strong buying intent, others much earlier in that journey, but still with great potential, and suggests what you may want to do next.

Level	Action	Appropriate Response
1	Had a sales meeting/discovery call and was very positive but not yet made a purchase	Follow up within 24 h to check in and agree next steps and follow up promptly until a buying decision is reached
2	Submitted application form or inquiry or questions prior to making a purchase	Follow up within 24 h to check in and agree next steps and follow up promptly until a buying decision is reached or offer a call to discuss next steps
3	Attended your free event or training	Personal follow-up to thank them and ask how they enjoyed the training
4	Downloaded a free piece of content	Nurture sequence and tailored offer or personal follow-up to thank them and welcome them, ask how they enjoyed the content
5	Met you at networking or event and expressed an interest	Follow up with a message or call and discuss next steps – could be straight to agreeing logistics, or inviting to a call, or inviting to an event, or signposting to an appropriate resource
6	Actively engaging with your social media content, opening emails, clicking links	Open a conversation, reach out to see if you can help, answer questions or discuss interest in a specific event or offer
7	New social media follower or connection	Welcome message and open a conversation. If appropriate, offer free content to get them onto your email list if that is the next step in your customer journey

How to Find Leads

Lead generation is getting people to raise their hand and say yes, I am potentially interested in this specific result/outcome/solution or benefit that your product or service offers. Then you can follow up with an appropriate offer or next step.

Lead generation isn't a one-off task; it's a daily commitment. Just like a bricks and mortar business wouldn't open only once a week, your online presence requires daily nurturing.

It is always a two-part process:

1. Look at buying intent signals and also subtler buying signals all around you and in every part of your business now and over the last three to six months (go back further if you need to) from people who are already in your world. They might be on your social media accounts, your email list, your mind, your inbox, new contacts at events, etc.
2. Do the work daily to generate brand-new leads.

Finding Existing Leads

Leads tend not to convert instantly so it is really important to track them so you can manage them through the process and keep in touch until they do convert which might be that day, the next week, next month or even next year.

It is another example of why long-term thinking and building for the long term is so important. If someone doesn't convert immediately, lots of business owners go out and try to get in front of more new people... and repeat. It represents such missed opportunity with all of these people, who just needed more time to get to know, like and trust you and be interested in your offer before they bought.

You can download my leads tracker and start to track your leads. It is free to you as a reader of this book. Just go to www.annapayne.online/book and download your tracker.

Once you have your tracker, start to populate it with people who are already in your ecosystem.

All around you are people who are interested, who are waiting to be helped and who may want to buy from us. These people are giving us subtle buying signals. As a successful business owner you need to tune in to these potential clients' signals so you can convert that interest into sales.

Look at it from a client experience perspective. People love to feel welcomed, invited, looked after and personally 'chosen', so connecting with these leads will not only drive results in your business, but will feel good for your clients too.

Let's start. I challenge you to find one hundred leads in your world already. If you can get to one hundred, that's great; if you can't just yet, that's fine. Get as far as you can, and later in the book you can look at generating new leads.

So grab the leads tracker at www.annapayne.online/book or even just a notepad and start writing your list of names. Think about these questions and try to come up with multiple names for each category.

1. Who do you have a feeling will work with you – they are interested – but hasn't bought yet?

2. Who do you know that you could ask for referrals? Clients, family, friends?
3. Previous clients you know you could work with again?
4. Previous client you could ask for referrals?
5. Potential partners (affiliates) who serve the same audience as you but offer something different – can you create a partnership with them?
6. Which of your current clients can you upsell something additional to?
7. What communities are you in with people that you could reach out to? E.g. Facebook groups, masterminds, memberships.
8. What new communities of your ideal clients can you get into?
9. Go to Instagram and Facebook – who is watching your stories but isn't a current client?
10. Who has followed you or connected with you on social media but you haven't yet spoken to or haven't spoken to recently?
11. Email marketing – who opens every email (maybe multiple times) and clicks through to what you have for sale or ways to work with you?
12. Who has downloaded your lead magnet?
13. Do you have a free community? Who are your most engaged members? Who has joined recently?
14. Do you have a podcast? Who is subscribed? Who has left you a fabulous review?
15. Who comments on your articles or blogs?
16. Who shares your content?

17. Who has inquired in the last twelve months but not bought?
18. Who have you sent proposals or information to that hasn't bought?
19. Networking: who have you met in person at events that expressed an interest in working with you?
20. What networking events can you attend, or pitch yourself as a guest speaker at?
21. Previous challenges and launches/freebies – who engaged?
22. Who has bought one of your low-price offers?
23. Who in your audience is a potential collaborator or connector?
24. Who are your best clients that you know may be ready to buy more?
25. Who has bought from you before but you haven't heard from in a while?
26. Who else can you think of in your world who is not a current client and you think should be?

Write all these names on your tracker. How many leads do you have? This exercise (I hope) will show you that the opportunity for sales is all around!

The first time you do this may feel difficult but hopefully the names will start to flow. Keep repeating this exercise regularly (at least weekly) and soon it will start to become natural. You'll pull out your phone frequently to add people to your leads list, ready to follow up!

You can come from the perspective of sales being hard, sales being lacking, and there are never enough people who want what you offer. Or you can see that when you look more carefully, opportunities are all around you. Grasp those opportunities and take action to convert them into results.

* * *

Takeaway: You haven't even looked yet at new people that don't know you, but I hope you already have a sizable list to follow up with.

It is far easier (and a better ROI) to convert people who already know you a little. You have done the work to bring them into your world, so forgetting about them is such a wasted effort.

Focus some attention and effort here to make these potential customers feel looked after and valued. This will certainly lead to more sales.

* * *

How Many Leads?

How many leads you need will depend on your offer suite. If you sell at a higher price and lower volume, you may only need five sales a month to hit your goals, in which case having thirty leads may be more than ample. If you want thirty sales, you might want one or two hundred leads.

If you want one thousand sales or more, unless you have a big team, you probably need a slightly different approach. Instead of tracking thousands of names, you can track your current and desired traffic sources and partnerships to get you that volume of leads.

Use your goals and desired outcomes along with your typical conversion rate to work out how many leads you want, and what type of leads you want. Then go out and get them!

*As a rule of thumb, I try to always have one hundred leads on my leads tracker. This evolves constantly as I work to sort them into Yes, No, or Maybe in the future in terms of sales. Your leads tracker isn't static; it should be changing daily/weekly. When it is a long list with one hundred names or more, I might slow down a little on the lead generation and do more following up.

When it is a shorter list, I know I have to ramp up lead generation.

Once people are on your leads tracker, you want to reach out to them to either open a conversation, to follow up with them, to draw an existing conversation to conclusion or to discuss next steps. More on that in the next section.

For now, I will help you explore ways to bring in more leads and inquiries.

Generating New Leads

Once you have identified your existing leads you will also want to get some fresh leads in. These might be leads who are already aware of you, or these might be brand new leads.

Take this action. Create four social media posts and schedule them for the next week. Watch closely which one drives the best engagement and results. When you know what works, you can lean further into it.

Although your core messages should stay consistent, different people are drawn in by different types of content and different hooks. What resonates with one person might not with another person. Constantly test and measure different headlines, questions versus statements, direct sales posts versus storytelling, and directing leads to freebies versus leads to paid offer lead generation.

Pay attention the whole time to what works and what brings in leads so you can amplify what works and then rinse and repeat.

Don't be afraid to experiment and play around with this. Have some fun doing it. Everything you do will be helpful. No one ever broke their business with marketing or sales!

Your Four Posts to Schedule This Week

Post 1 - A Story Post: Your Story

Write a proper story with an engaging beginning, a middle and an end. It could be about how you got started in business, a time you felt stuck, what you are most proud of, why you do what you do, a challenging time...

Remember to add a call to action. It could be one that encourages engagement, asking people to drop you a GIF below if they agree, comment if this ever happened to them or if they resonate, or asking a relevant and easy to answer question. Or it could be more sales focused, asking them to click here to learn more or drop you an emoji below and you'll send the info.

Post 2 - Reviews / Social Proof

Share a testimonial, review, case study or even your own story of transformation – even better if you can back this up with visuals.

Add a call to action to comment below or DM you a specific word if they'd like to find out how you can help them achieve this result.

Post 3 - Ladder Post

Get people to raise their hands if they are interested. E.g. *'I have noticed a lot of (insert ideal client) are struggling with (x) right now and really want to do (y) so they can (z).*

If this is you, I have the perfect thing for you coming up. Then a direct call to action could be, *'Drop me an emoji in the comments, comment below, like this post, DM me, or click here to learn more.*

Post 4 - Direct Sales Post: Yes, Yes, Yes!

This is similar to above but asking questions to get your ideal client to answer yes with regard to benefits, transformations and solutions. So...

Do you x?

Are you y?

Would you really like to be z?

Focus on areas such as how it will make them feel, how it will make their life easier/better/happier/healthier? What is the result? Why is this better than what they have tried before? Then use a direct call to action, e.g. *'Click here to buy, book a call, message me a keyword to get the details.'*

As you try these types of post:

1. Notice which works best for you. Which are people most engaged with?
2. Use your knowledge of your ideal client to really speak to them.
3. Focus not just on the what or the how but on the why.
4. Consider how you want people to feel.
5. Share great images.
6. Respond appropriately to people who engage and add them to your leads list for follow-up.

Conversations

Starting new and meaningful conversations with relevant people is one of the simplest yet most overlooked strategies to build relationships and develop leads.

It is not as sophisticated as a sales funnel, but to me it is the base of everything you do. Adding funnels, automations and email sequences that's great, but it should all be underpinned and enhanced by the basic skill of conversation.

I don't mean a cold spammy DM that asks an annoying and irrelevant question, says *buy my thing* or *join my challenge* or *book a call*. You aren't trying to get the person to buy anything at this stage. They aren't ready. It is a brand new relationship so be mindful of that in the way you engage. The messages should be personalised, friendly and relevant.

I try to start at least ten new conversations a day. Not everyone will reply straight away, and that's ok. I focus my energy on the people who do reply.

These conversations could be with anyone you have identified as a lead.

- Opening emails and clicking links
- Engaging with social content
- New social media follower
- Recently downloaded free training or low-cost offer
- Past client
- Someone you want to collaborate with
- Existing client with potential to work more closely with
- Someone you met at networking
- Someone you connected with online but don't really know

The exact message you send will depend on who the person is, whether you know them, and how far along the customer journey they are. If they are a brand new contact, be very brief and friendly and give value without asking for anything in return.

One example of this is to start conversations with new followers or social media connections. That usually looks like:

Hi (first name), Thanks so much for connecting here. I really appreciate you following me and I hope you enjoy my approach to sales and business growth.

Now I can insert anything relevant such as:

- I see you are based in Edinburgh... me too. Do you attend many networking events?
- I love your branding/product/message. It really speaks to me!

I could ask an easy question (easy because we want it to be easy for them to answer!)

- Are you looking for any support when it comes to sales?
- Do you have any questions about my business?

And/or I can have a call to action which might be any of the following:

- As a welcome gift I have some free resources to help business owners make more sales which you can find here at www.annapayne.online/everything if you'd like to take a look and grab whatever you need.
- So nice to connect with you. Let's keep in touch and I look forward to chatting more.

- I thought I'd let you know I have a free challenge coming up soon to help business owners make more sales. Would you like me to send you the details?
- I run monthly networking for entrepreneurs. Let me know if you'd like to come along and try one.

More Ways to Generate Leads

- Leveraging other people's audiences by appearing in front of them as a guest. Give them something that pulls them into your world, such as a free gift/lead magnet to get them onto your email list.
- Networking
- Conversations
- Quizzes
- Challenges
- Discount codes
- Competitions
- Brochures or price lists
- Books
- Podcasts
- Free or very low-cost offers
- Lead magnets like PDFs, Checklists, Templates, Tools, Ebooks

It is great to have these tools to generate leads but you also need to consistently tell people you have them and point them towards them!

Leveraging Other People's Audiences

You can certainly build your own audience, but 'borrowing' other people's has lots of benefits. It accelerates your audience growth and lead generation strategies.

If you are a coach, consultant or service provider, leveraging other people's audiences to offer guest expert training is a highly effective lead generation strategy. This allows you to tap into established communities, reaching potential clients who are already interested in your area of expertise. It's a win-win situation: you provide valuable content and, in return, gain exposure to a wider audience. Have a compelling offer or call to action for them at the end.

One of the key reasons this strategy works so well is that it builds trust and credibility. When you are introduced as a trusted expert and authority on your subject, this is an endorsement from the host. Your host is trusted by their audience and this trust transfers to you, making them warmer and more receptive to your message. (Caution: be careful who you trust with your audience and who you partner with. Aligned values and integrity matter.)

This approach is cost-effective as it costs you only your time, rather than paid ad spend. Plus, these sessions provide an opportunity for direct interaction with potential leads, allowing you to establish personal connections that can lead to long-term business relationships. It can be a game-changer.

There are several other effective ways to leverage others' audiences.

- Collaborations are powerful. By partnering with another business or expert, you can double your potential reach *and* give your audience something extra. I love partnering with others who serve the same clients and have the same end goals but help them in a different yet complementary way to me. Not only do I meet lots of great new people, I know the clients get great value too.
- You may wish to offer an affiliate programme to other businesses or individuals to promote your services. This approach extends your reach and again builds trust instantly, which can be highly persuasive.
- Contributing articles or blog posts to online summits and bundles can also be beneficial. This allows you to showcase your expertise to a new audience.
- Podcast guesting is another great strategy. You get a chance to speak directly to an engaged and targeted audience. You can share your story, expertise, and insights in a more personal and relatable way. This format allows for a deeper connection with listeners, as they get to hear your voice and understand your passion and expertise firsthand. It is also an opportunity to discuss complex topics in a more digestible and engaging manner, which can be more effective than written content.
- Additionally, podcast episodes have a longer shelf life than other forms of media and can continue to generate leads and interest for a long time.

However you decide to collaborate and leverage others' audiences:

1. Be clear on the value you bring so that when you ask to collaborate it is an easy yes.
2. Don't wait to be invited. Knock on doors and ask to be considered for these opportunities.
3. Give value and always have an appropriate call to action, usually a free resource or tool which brings them straight onto your email list is the best strategy so long as your host is happy with you offering that at the end.

Some More Social Media Posts to Generate Leads

In amongst your value, your authority and your know, like and trust posts, don't forget the importance of regular posts that are either direct sales or that generate leads for your business. By regular, think daily, or at least a few times a week, not monthly or quarterly.

To make it easy, I have listed some small but mighty social media posts to generate leads and inquiries every time you hit 'post'.

Post them as they are, or, even better, tweak them to sound more like your tone of voice. Fill in the blanks using the very words your ideal clients use to describe their own goals, wants and needs. (Benefits not features!)

Don't overthink it, and have fun experimenting to see which language and which posts attract the greatest results for your audience.

Remember to track your leads so you can follow up with them.

1. The Yes Method

Hey online service providers, would you like to wake up to an inbox full of inquiries?

- *Dreaming of payment notifications buzzing your phone?*
- *Want to make consistent sales?*
- *Want to attract your dream clients with ease?*

If you nodded 'yes' to the above, drop an emoji below. I've got something that will help you achieve just that!

2. The X1Z30

Amazing results alert! My fantastic client, Jess, just made over £12k in eight weeks with our new sales strategy.

Want success like Jess? I've got space for two smart, hard-working and ambitious coaches to work closely with me using my VALUE sales framework to radically increase their sales and income over the next ninety days. I want to take you from £2k months to £10k months. Interested? DM 'VALUE' for details!

3. Challenge Sign-Up

Do you want to turn your Instagram into a money making machine instead of a drain on your time, creating hours and hours of content with no results? Transform your [specific topic, e.g., 'Instagram engagement'] in just five days! Join our free Instagram Insiders acceleration challenge and see the difference in your engagement and results. Click the link or comment 'I'm IN' to sign up! #5DayTransformChallenge

4. Downloadable Guide Offer

Master the art of [specific topic, e.g., 'email marketing'] so you can (insert desired outcome). Get your hands on my in-depth guide, loaded with tips and tricks and insider info to save you time and hassle and get you making more money from your email list. Want a copy? Simply comment 'Yes' below!

5. Exclusive Webinar

Save the date! I've made £10k+ from one sales funnel in the last thirty days. Join me live next Thursday as I delve deep into [topic, e.g., 'effective sales funnels']. If sales on repeat, every day, even while you sleep sounds appealing, let's make it happen! Comment 'REMIND ME' to secure your spot!

6. Behind-the-Scenes Teaser

"Something exciting is brewing! Here's a sneak peek [attach teaser image/video]. Can you guess what it is? If you're as excited as I am, drop a gif in the comments and I'll add you to my list for exclusive early info!

7. Personalised Quiz Feedback

"How effective is your [specific, e.g., 'sales strategy']? Take my FREE two-minute quiz and get expert feedback tailored just for you to show up your biggest opportunities and uncover any blind spots. Go to www.annapayne.online/quiz now to get started!

8. Join the Exclusive Club

"Big news! I'm launching a brand new community for dedicated [target audience, e.g., 'entrepreneurs'] who want to [insert desired outcome]. Limited founder slots available now. Comment 'VIP' if you're in!

10. Flash Offer

Surprise! For the next 24 hours, I've opened up my diary to offer five one-on-ones [e.g. 'marketing audit'] for those serious about levelling up their marketing this year. Strictly limited to five slots and at the ridiculous price of £149! (Normally working with me starts from £1000.) So if you've been wanting to work with me for a while, now is the time. Drop a 'yes' to grab this chance!

11. Share Your Journey

"From [past struggle, e.g., 'zero clients'] to [current achievement, e.g., 'a fully booked business charging premium prices'] in one year. Want to know the five very specific things I did to get there? Ready to do the same? Comment 'I'm ready' and I'll share the short training on it!

12. Epic Collaboration Teaser

Something BIG is coming! Teaming up with [expert name] to bring you [benefit, e.g., 'cutting-edge marketing strategies']. Want to know what's going on? Comment 'Me' for a special preview!

13. Are You Ready?

Are you ready to [insert specific outcome or result e.g. launch your podcast/online course / run an event/ earn extra £1500 per month/ sign three new clients/ save time/save money/save hassle/lose 10kgs etc.] in the next 1/3/6 months?

Comment 'I'm Ready'

14. Feedback Loop Offer:

I need YOU! I'm looking for ten entrepreneurs who have been in business for two years plus and want to scale to six-figures in the next year to be part of a case study group I am putting together. Not only will you get hugely discounted access, you'll also have my full attention as we work to create amazing results. Click here to apply/learn more.

15. Success Stories Showcase:

Success Spotlight! Meet [Client's Name], who went from [challenge] to [success in just two months] as part of my momentum programme. Inspired? Want to be my next success story? Click here to book a free 15-minute consultation call and let's chat about how we can help you create results like this.

16. Engaging Poll:

"Debate time! When it comes to [specific topic], do you believe [Option A] or [Option B] is more crucial for success? Cast your vote! And if you're curious about what my data says, drop your best curious GIF below and I'll share the results via DM tomorrow'.

17. Product Development Poll:

I'm deep in the creation phase for my next product and need YOUR insights! Which feature would you love to see? A) or B)? Cast your vote! Those who participate will get a very special thank you offer when I launch!

18. Training Topics Poll:

"I'm planning my next training session and want to tailor it to YOUR needs. What topic would benefit you the most? A) or B) Let me know and I'll save you a free spot on the training.

20. Industry Trend Poll:

[Your Industry, e.g., 'digital marketing'] is always evolving. What trend are you most curious about for the coming year? A) or B)? Share your thoughts, and I'll be breaking down my views on the top-voted trend in my next live session!

Part 5

Unlock Sales

Vision: Define your goals and set targets for a clear, focused approach.

Audience: Get visible with a clear, compelling message to build your audience.

Lead Generation: Take daily action to generate and nurture leads.

Unlock sales: Make compelling offers and convert leads into sales.

Excellence: Deliver with excellence and leverage your success.

Chapter 15

Crafting Your Irresistible Offers

You might already feel that by implementing everything you've read, you are covering more than you are used to in terms of selling. If you implement it all consistently, for sure you'll see an upturn in your results.

But here is the exciting part; there is so much more you can do to influence outcomes and convert your leads into sales than waiting and seeing what happens from here on in. That looks like:

- Valuable offer(s) based on your ideal clients' most pressing wants and needs
- A clear value proposition for each offer
- Clear and confident pricing
- Understanding the psychology of sales
- A plan to present these offers to prospective buyers
- Asking for the sale
- Following up

Doing the tasks and applying the strategies you are about to read about will help your business stand out to your clients and potential clients for all the right reasons. It will put you ahead of most others in your industry (because most people don't do any of this).

Before we get into the nitty gritty of unlocking sales, let's get clear on your offers. then we'll look at how you can sell more of them, and then we'll close out this section with some notes on pricing. Lack of clarity around offer or confusion over pricing can be a real hindrance to your sales success, so let's nail these parts down.

Creating Offers That Sell

There is no point in developing a product or service no one wants to buy, yet many businesses decide what to offer, then hope to find a market for it afterwards.

Successful companies find out what customers need or want and then develop the right product with the right level of quality to meet their expectations, both now and in the future.

When I was twenty I worked a summer season on Crete and did a variety of casual jobs for a few drachmas a day. My first job was working at a pool bar, selling iced coffees, cold drinks and frozen smoothies. I didn't need to sell the benefits of these drinks. People queued up because they knew they wanted and needed them and they were the obvious choice.

You want to be the obvious choice. Alex Hormozi talks about creating offers so good that people feel stupid saying no. I want you to feel that your offers are so good, not only can you not stop talking about them, but actually they are really compelling. People should want them and know they need them. You don't have to spend a lot of time explaining or convincing them. If you find this is the case, you need to go back to the drawing board and figure out what your audience actually wants.

Valuable, Specific, Client-centred Offers

Good offers are about solving people's problems and making life easier and better for them. You looked at how to convey that in your over-arching messaging. But if you sell multiple offers, you need messaging and a clear value proposition around each of the things you offer. Communicate what you do with clarity and in terms of the problems, goals and aspirations of your ideal clients.

Your product or service bridges the gap from point A (current state) to point B (desired outcome) for your clients. You should now be crystal clear on your clients' journey and what both points A and B look and *feel* like for your clients. Refer to this journey/transformation/solution and *why* it matters (direct and indirect benefits) consistently.

Doing this means your offer resonates deeply and emotionally with the people who need your help and help them to understand why what you do matters to them. This approach is much more likely to trigger a sale.

Always ask, what does your audience really want and need right now? What is a must have for them? How do they feel about this? How can you talk about it in terms of benefits?

For example:

- If you sell beds, no one really pays for a mattress, they pay for the best possible night's sleep. Perhaps their bed is so old they have broken sleep every night, which makes them tired and irritable in every day. They don't perform well at work and they skip their morning workouts because they are so shattered. Maybe they have a nagging backache due to their saggy old mattress. No wonder they are ready to invest in an improved night's sleep which they hope will make them happier, healthier, more energised and a better parent, partner and employee.

- If you are a coach, no one *wants* to buy a coaching package, they want to buy the transformation and growth you facilitate. The coaching package is just the vehicle to get them there, just like the spring count, memory foam, cooling gel and cashmere topper are just vehicles to achieve a better night's sleep and all the benefits that brings.

Be clear on what people's buying triggers are, and what they want and need. Then elevate that to understanding why that matters to them, and also how they feel to be where they are now. So much of sales is about feelings and emotions.

The best thing you can do to get clear on this is to do market research upfront. Then if you sell one to one, remember, do not make assumptions. Ask, don't tell. If you are in a sales conversation with someone, ask them lots of questions so you can respond based on the facts, not your assumptions.

Why are you interested in this?

What about this appeals to you?

What sort of outcome/benefit are you looking for?

Why have you chosen to look now?

Why me/this offer/this product?

Which other offers are you considering right now?

Ask as many open questions as you need to draw people out and into a conversation where you can then understand more deeply what they want and need and respond appropriately.

Understanding Sales Psychology

Sales psychology is a blend of understanding your customers' emotions and logical reasoning. It revolves around understanding what triggers a potential customer to make a purchase. These triggers can be broadly categorised into emotional and logical buying triggers, each playing a crucial role in influencing customer decisions. When you add value, trust and urgency to the mix you have a really compelling offer.

The best offers should have:

1. **A clear value proposition,** i.e. you can explain in simple terms why people should buy it and how it will make their lives easier or happier, how it will help them be healthier, wealthier, happier, or save them time or money.

2. **Emotional impact:** We are emotional beings, and it is emotion which usually first attracts a prospect's attention. They can be positive or negative emotions. I tend to lead with positive emotions as I want to attract action takers who are aspirational. For some industries, 'pain-point' messaging may be more applicable. Emotional triggers tap into feelings such as desire, fear, happiness, or a sense of belonging. For instance, a customer might buy a luxury car or a designer pair of shoes, not for functionality but for the prestige and status and how they boost their self-esteem.

3. **Logical Buying Triggers:** Logical triggers, on the other hand, appeal to the customer's sense of reasoning and practicality. These include factors like product features, cost-effectiveness, dates, details, and usefulness. A customer might choose a phone with an extra long battery life or a fabulous camera over brand loyalty, so they make a decision based on logical assessment.

4. **Trust and Credibility:** Trust and credibility are crucial in sales psychology. Customers are eighty percent more likely to purchase from a brand or individual they trust. Building trust can involve

demonstrating expertise, providing excellent customer service, and ensuring product quality. Credibility can be established through customer reviews, consistent brand messaging, and guarantees.

5. **Urgency:** When clients tell me about their fabulous offers and why people should buy them, my next question is why should they buy it *now?* How can you use genuine urgency (not false!) to prompt immediate action? Sometimes it can be very simple as there is limited availability or something happens on a specific date or time, but you may need to get more creative and use dynamic pricing, time-limited bonuses, and exclusive deals. However, use this tactic with integrity and sparingly, to avoid scepticism.

Your Actions

- **Emotional Triggers:** What emotions drive your clients' behaviour? How can your product or service connect emotionally?
- **The Decision-making Process:** How does your ideal client make purchasing decisions? What factors are most influential?
- **Trust and Credibility Factors:** What builds trust and credibility with your audience? How can you get more compelling testimonials, and share these? What else can you do to build trust?

- **Urgency:** Are you using urgency to drive sales? What might you add to use this where applicable?

Chapter 16

Actions to Drive Sales and Conversions

Ask For the Sale

Now you know your offers are great and you've generated some leads (woo-hoo). Don't stop now. Get out there and ask for the sale/make the offer:

You can do this in a number of ways. It could be a social media post or an email with a direct call to action to click to buy or book now. Maybe it is an online sales page. Or perhaps you ask face to face or on the phone, or at a masterclass or webinar where you give value and sell to lots of people at a time.

Ask for the sale and make sure you are easy to buy from. Make it very clear what the customer needs to do next at every stage of the journey. Make it is as smooth, simple and frictionless as possible for them to get to the point of buying.

Do you ask for the sale? Most people don't; they present the information and then kind of wait awkwardly. Some people might buy at this point but others need more encouragement.

This important opportunity, while seemingly straightforward, is where many sales conversations falter. Approach it with confidence, knowing that you and your marketing and lead generation efforts have laid the groundwork to receive as many positive responses as possible at this time.

Here are some key points to help you ask for the sale:

Build a Solid Foundation: Before you even think of asking them to buy, establish rapport. You should also understand your potential clients' needs, wants and pain points, and make sure that you're not making any assumptions, either positive or negative.

Inform: Your potential client should have the details they need about your product or service. Highlight the benefits and how it solves their specific problems. An informed client is more likely to make a positive decision.

Read the Room: Pay attention to the client's cues. Are they engaged? Do they seem interested or are they hesitant or non-committal? Tailor your next steps based on their reactions. If they seem hesitant, try to establish and address their concerns. If they are very engaged, it might be the right time to move forward.

The Art of Asking: The actual ask should be clear and direct, yet unobtrusive. Phrases like, 'How does this sound to you?' or, 'Are you interested in going ahead?' are effective. They prompt a response without putting pressure on the client.

Expect Objections: Be prepared for objections. They're not always straight rejections, but sometimes just opportunities to address their concerns. But also don't feel you have to combat or argue. If someone tells me they can't afford something, or they want to discuss it with their partner, I will not try to push them forward. I'll just say, *'Yes, great idea. It is so important that you do that because I understand it's a big investment and you want to be certain. Please discuss it with your partner and then I'll call you tomorrow and we can pick up from there.'*

Or I say, *'Of course, if that price point isn't accessible right now, would you like me to look at a payment plan for you? Or would you feel more comfortable having a look at a lower-priced product or service? I have a low-cost membership that might be a great place for you to get started. Shall I tell you about that?'*

Asking for the Sale

If you sell face to face or on the phone, get used to asking for the sale. Use an approach that feels natural, human and respectful of your clients' decision-making processes.

Here are some approaches to try out:

Direct Approach: Simply ask, 'Are you ready to get started with [service/package]?' This straightforward question is clear and direct, making it easy for the client to decide.

Option Close: Offer choices such as, "Would you prefer the standard or VIP Upgrade package?' By providing options, you're assuming the sale and gently nudging the client to make a choice. I know lots of people use this, although I don't love it for my business. To me it feels pushy but it does work in some settings. See how it feels for you.

Soft Close: Use softer language, like, 'How do you feel about moving forward with this?' This approach is less pushy and allows the client to express their thoughts or concerns. This is usually more my speed.

Summary Close: Summarise the benefits and value of your service, then ask, 'Does this sound like what you're looking for?' This method reinforces the value proposition and leads into the closing question.

Urgency Close: If applicable, create a sense of urgency, 'The price point or bonus pack changes after today, so do you want to go ahead now?' or, 'This is my last spot until next year; would you like it?' This method can motivate clients to act quickly but has to be done with integrity.

Trial Close: Test the waters with a question like, 'Does this sound like it has everything you need?' 'Does everything make sense so far?' or, 'Do you have any other questions?' This can help gauge their readiness to buy.

Results Close: Asking, 'Would you like me to support you in achieving [goal]?' can be effective, as it positions the sale as the logical next step for them to solve their problems and achieve their goals.

Please don't ever try to close a sale reading from a script. Funnily enough, that tends not to work!

Keep it natural, friendly and focused on getting to the right resolution. Sales conversations should feel comfortable and natural for both parties.

Ask for the sale. One of four things will happen:

1. **The Worst-case Scenario:** They say *no I'm never buying, I don't like this thing and I don't like you. Go away.* This is rare and if you do your nurturing and qualification correctly, it will hardly ever happen. I don't want to jinx myself but I can't remember the last time I had this kind of response. This is because I do the groundwork and I don't make offers until people have expressed an interest, given permission and are ready to buy. If it does happen to you, it isn't a negative, just a statistic; only a certain proportion of people will say yes. Just expect upfront that you will get some nos. Decide for each 'no' whether you can learn anything from it. If you can use it to refine your process and move on, it is statistically speaking one step closer to a yes.

2. **The Ghost:** They don't reply to you or answer you. For me this is the worst-case scenario. I'd rather someone just said *no, go away* than ignore me and I waste time following up, waiting and wondering. If someone ghosts you don't assume it's on purpose. It is much more likely they are busy, they forgot or life got in the way. This happens to me frequently when I am in the buying position so I appreciate a gentle nudge. I think if you have had previous conversations it is perfectly valid to follow up several

times before you cut off communication and assume it's a no for now.

3. **They say it's not right:** Either it is not the right offer, not the right time, or not the right price point, which opens up a conversation and allows you to work with them on finding the right solution which may result in a sale now or will be a lead to follow up on in the future.

4. **You make a sale! Hooray for the best possible outcome – go you!**

The Problem With 'Handling Objections'

I can barely write that phrase without cringing! *Handling objections*. Ewww. What kind of sales expert does that make me? It makes me the sort of sales expert who trusts customers to know their own minds and make decisions.

In the world of sales, the term 'handling objections' often conjures up images of pushy tactics and aggressive persuasion. Traditionally, sales training has focused on overcoming objections – a method which trains the seller to counteract resistance from the buyer, often with scripted responses. This can often feel forceful and inauthentic, leaving the customer feeling pressured. It not only undermines the seller's integrity but can also damage the long-term relationship with the customer. This approach can feel uncomfortable for both the seller and the buyer, is unlikely to deliver results, and usually leads to an experience that no one enjoys.

My view is that when you push people into things they aren't sure about, that causes a high rate of people who drop out, who cancel, who put in payment disputes, whose payments fail or who find other ways to get out of things. Making sales like this isn't a sound strategy and is an exhausting way to do business. You churn and burn through clients instead of building long-term partnerships and repeat customers.

* * *

Qualifying Your Sales

When I worked in recruitment, we used to place very senior doctors in jobs around the world, perhaps a Consultant Neurosurgeon moving from Edinburgh to Sydney or a Professor of Obstetrics moving from New York to Singapore... major moves that took a year or more to arrange, involve multiple regulatory bodies, visas, medical checks, and relocating entire families, pets, furniture, sometimes classic cars or windsurfers and all.

There was a lot of scope for things to go wrong and a lot of time for the candidate or the spouse or the kids to get cold feet, or for something to change such as an elderly parent who couldn't be left.

These were big deals worth a lot of money, with some fees worth up to around $50,000. If that candidate pulled out any time before the end of their first eight weeks of employment, we got paid nothing. *Zero!* A year or more of hard work to get nothing.

Attrition rate (drop out of placed candidates) was a key performance indicator for us: there was always going to be some drop out but we ideally wanted it to be under five percent, under ten percent at a push. Anything over ten percent was an issue.

We were incredibly thorough in qualifying a candidate's interest, in giving them time to think, in testing their commitment over and over again, and in exploring what might go wrong so that we only invested our time in the candidates who had the greatest level of commitment, not anyone who was having a bad day, was sick of the UK winter and fancied applying for a job at Bondi Beach but hadn't taken into account their spouse with a professional career, their kids sitting exams or their elderly parents who required daily visits.

I had new recruiters coming in all guns blazing, desperate to make money and I'd think wow, they've placed twenty candidates in three months and billed over £200k, only for eighteen of those twenty candidates to drop out over the next nine months and £180k to come out of our pipeline.

To be successful, we had to play the long game and think hard about qualifying sales, never pushing non-committed people to make purchases they didn't want.

When someone complains that all their clients are dropping out, defaulting on payments or withdrawing, I know it is probably an issue in the sales process. They have been persuaded into something rather than having made a committed decision.

Be the person who qualifies their prospects, who allows them to make their own decisions and, where relevant, acknowledges their objections rather than tries to bulldoze them.

An example of qualifying prospects is that if you book a discovery call with me to inquire about working one-to-one, you have to fill out some details and you will also have to tick a box to say you understand the pricing and are in a position to invest either in full or with a payment plan. If you don't already do this, start! It will save you so much time on discovery calls.

When you play the long game, people will remember you and thank you for it.

This leads me to the biggest investment to date I have ever made in a mastermind for my business. It was a big purchase. A lot of money. Money I didn't have at the time and I knew I would have to make more money every month to pay it off. It wasn't sold to me. I had to complete an application form. I think had a fifteen-minute call to see if I was a good fit and sell myself. Smart, right? Of course, I wanted to be selected and chosen.

* * *

If you don't want to handle objections, what alternative strategies represent a more genuine and more respectful approach to sales?

You Can Pre-handle Objections

Instead of waiting for objections to come up during the sales process, why not brainstorm the most likely or most frequent objections and address them beforehand? You can do this through your content and marketing. By anticipating potential concerns and addressing them in your marketing materials, you can clear doubts before they even arise. This proactive approach builds trust.

Another good way if you sell higher priced offers is to use bonuses or added value things that negate fears or doubts. For example, I ran a sales confidence programme some time ago. I know a lot of people didn't have the confidence to carry out some of the actions so as a bonus, I brought in a mindset coach.

My brand photographer client knows people can feel awkward and uncomfortable on shoots, or say there's no point as they never like the images of themselves that they get back. So on her VIP shoots she brings in the support of a Stylist and Hair and Make Up Artist and even a Visibility Expert to help people know that despite their misgivings, they will get the best results from the brand shoot.

People might have fears about whether what you do will be good enough. Give them a cast iron guarantee and share lots and lots of reviews.

Ask Open Questions

Asking open-ended questions is such a key part of good, consultative selling. By asking open questions such as what, why, who, when and how, you get engaged in a conversation where you better understand your potential clients needs, challenges and preferences. You can then tailor your offering to the customer's specific situation, making the sale feel more like a helpful consultation than a pushy pitch.

Be Flexible (if that works for you)

Sometimes, closing the sale isn't possible. Having alternative solutions, such as downsells, upsells (if they need more support) or flexible payment plans, can be really helpful. These options build trust and help you make more sales as well as potentially leading to future sales.

The key to successful sales isn't ever in pushing or forcing. It is about building trust and serving your customer's needs.

The most successful sales strategies are those that build lasting relationships based on trust and mutual benefit.

Chapter 17

Follow up With Your Leads

The first point of contact is important, of course. You never get a second chance to make a first impression. But too many people make the mistake of crafting a perfect sales email, holding a great meeting, or running a fantastic webinar or event, and then sitting back and doing nothing. Waiting for the sales to roll in.

If you do this, you are not alone. But I know you are not tapping into all the sales that are possible for you.

These statistics will highlight to you what a massive opportunity you have to hugely increase your results.

- **Only two percent of sales happen on the first offer**
- **Eighty percent of sales happen after five or more follow ups**
- **But forty-eight percent of business owners say they NEVER follow up**

- **Forty-four percent follow up once then stop**
- **Only ten percent say they follow up three or more times**

Take a moment to consider what this looks like. Imagine you attend a conference at a large hotel. You go into one room and find yourself with forty-seven other people in your industry and two buyers who are ready to buy. You might make a sale but the odds are that you won't. It is noisy, busy, maybe a bit shouty, and everyone is competing for attention. Your fellow business owners are all trying to get attention. You're pretty sure someone stood on your toes and someone else elbowed you. It is so noisy that if you're not the shouty type, you'll feel like just blending into the walls.

Now imagine there's another room you can earn entry to. That room has only nine other people in your industry plus eighty clients. They all are ready to buy and are literally waiting to speak to you, queuing up to get your attention so they can get what they need. I-t is likely that if you work smart and work quickly you will make multiple sales in this room.

Every day when you sit down to your work, remember these two rooms and decide which one you want to operate from. If it is the second one, the way to do that is to follow up with your leads! Doing this well and doing it consistently will distinguish you from almost everyone else in your industry. You straight away get to the top ten percent of salespeople with this one strategy.

Are you convinced?

Most people say, *'Yes, I hear you, but following up with my leads feels so pushy. What do I say?'*

What if we reframe that as helping people? Giving better service?

I know how busy my life is. I have two kids with about twenty activities between them, a husband, a dog, plus two businesses. My head is quite often spinning with meetings, deadlines, projects and goals whilst also trying to remember to order school lunches, rebook football classes, book the dog in for her vaccinations, and then thinking I'd love some help with x... maybe I could get more admin support from an extra VA... and I also need to book the dentist, get my eyebrows waxed and my nails done, book our holiday, book that table for our night out this weekend and get the car in for its MOT. I also want someone to give me a quote for new blinds and for painting the living room. And on it goes.

It is entirely possible I will send a message in the evening or over the weekend when I have time. I don't get a reply until the next work day. If that reply comes in when I have a day of meetings and I can't answer, by the end of the day it is buried under about thirty messages and alerts and my diary is full. I will most likely forget and then remember again at some point in the future and repeat the whole cycle!

I appreciate a reminder or two, or three, to ask if I have any questions, to send me the link to book, or ask me if I want to go ahead. I never see that as pushy, I see it as really helpful.

I only see it as pushy and annoying when:

1. Someone who sends me a cold, unsolicited message that is clearly copy-and-paste and is not relevant to me or my business.
2. I've already said no thank you, but someone won't take no for an answer.

If you do not do either of these things, you are fine to follow up. It is a way to strengthen relationships, build trust, understand people, and help people. Of course, all of this leads to more sales. Everyone's a winner!

* * *

How Does This Look in Practice?

Every month in my membership we run a live implementation session and follow up with our leads. Every single call we get multiple people making sales either because someone had a simple question that was answered quickly, someone had forgotten and been meaning to buy, or someone just clicks the link and buys.

It is very exciting and every month reinforces to my members that this works.

Here are some examples for you:

1. A HAPPY STORY: Someone who had spent a lot of time with two clients on a consultation agreed to send the proposal with it being a done deal. Two

weeks later she had heard *nothing* back. She was gutted and a bit annoyed, thinking the clients were time-wasters. She followed up with them and lo and behold the proposal had gone straight to junk. It had not been seen. She was frustrated that the clients were time-wasters; on the other side the clients were disappointed that she hadn't followed up. A quick DM, it was sorted and the sale was done. Win-win.

2. A SAD STORY: Last year I had a huge number of emails in four mailboxes and it was overwhelming. Someone was recommended to me who, for a fixed price, would come in and sort everything, unsubscribe me from things and set up rules to organise my inbox. I messaged her, and we agreed on a price and a date to get it done. However, two days later instead of invoicing me she said she wanted to do a discovery call to see the scope of work, which was fine. I booked that in and her next availability matching mine was about three weeks away. Then we got an email to say the school nativity play was happening at that exact time. (Our school likes to spring things on us!) I cancelled the appointment and asked to chat over messages and voice notes to move things forward. She sent me her diary link to book another call which I just did not have time to do. It got to the Christmas holidays, I hadn't done it, and I never heard from her again. She may have made a conscious decision not to work with me, and if so that's fine, but I don't think so. Our communications were really friendly and I

would have happily paid for that service. If it had gone well, I'd almost certainly have had other ongoing work but because she wasn't straightforward to buy from, and she never followed up, nothing went ahead. If your service is all about supporting busy people with admin, you know your clients need help and are definitely busy. Following up and making the sales process easy is an essential part of driving sales.

3. **A Success Story:** I did a challenge launch a few years back with a group of around one hundred people. At the end of the challenge I taught a free masterclass and opened cart on my programme. My target was fifteen to twenty sales. Three people bought within the first five minutes and I was blown away. We were going away for a long weekend and the sales were going to come rolling in. Four days later, I still had three sales. I set about messaging everyone who had taken part in the challenge, starting with the most active and engaged people. The messages were personalised where appropriate but went something like, *'Hey Anna, thank you so much for taking part in my Sales Sprint this week. It's been great to see you taking action and getting results already. Did you see my Sales Confidence group programme starts next week? Are you thinking of joining us? I think you'd be such a great fit and I'd love to carry on working with you. Enrolment closes at the end of the week, so please let me know if you have any questions.'* I ended that with fifteen fabulous people in my programme. So

following up multiplied my results by five. This type of follow up is part of every launch I do.

Being consistent with your follow-up increases your chances of converting leads into customers. On a human scale it makes people feel valued, taken care of and like they are receiving great service.

---

* * *

Who to Follow up With?

I don't agree with cold messaging in most situations, as I don't think it's effective, (unless you are selling b2b rather than to individuals or small businesses, in which case you probably want to make a direct approach in addition to the strategies I am sharing here).

Instead, invest the time in creating conversations with people who are already on the outskirts of your world, and draw them in closer. I don't just follow up with leads where we have had specific sales conversations. I also follow up or start conversations with:

- People who have recently bought
- Existing customers
- Lapsed customers
- People I want to collaborate with

- People I have met at networking or events
- New social media followers
- People who have downloaded my free training or very low-cost offers
- People who have given buying signals
- People who are really engaged on my social media
- People who are really engaged on my email list

At the start of each week I braindump who I want to connect with, follow up with and start a conversation with and they go on my leads tracker (grab your free copy at www.anna payne.online/book). I work on that through the week, adding new people as new leads come in.

I always start with the 'warmest' leads but I am also conscious of starting new conversations so that when warm leads convert, there are more to replace them.

Earlier I asked you to create your first leads list so this is exactly where to start. I also suggested posting some lead generating content, so you can respond to everyone who engaged with that.

What Should You Say in a Follow-Up?

- **Be personal:** Sure, have some standard versions of messages you send, but these should not be a straight copy-and-paste. Use someone's name. (I have an irrational hatred of messages that start with *hey, girl.*)

- Reference previous interactions so people know why you are contacting them and it doesn't appear to be a cold message. *We met last week at xx event.*
- Know why you are reaching out to them.
- Explain the reason you are getting in touch - it could be, *I remember you told me you wanted X. I have something coming out later this month that is going to help people do X. I thought of you straight away - shall I send you the details?* Or it might be *I've been thinking about you,* or *I keep seeing you everywhere online and it prompted me to message you!*
- Provide value, like a helpful resource, a special discount, a preview, or even just some warmth and encouragement.
- Be Clear and concise – no one wants paragraphs in the DMs or four-minute voice notes.
- Call to action. What do you want them to do next? Schedule a call? Visit your website? Reply to you? Let them know.

I think conversations should be nuanced, natural and personalised so I haven't included loads of scripts but here are some examples that might help you.

After an Initial Inquiry:

- *Thank you so much for your interest in [Product/Service]. Let me know if you've any questions at this stage. I also thought you might find this [article/eBook/blog/review/case*

*study/social media post] about [relevant topic]
helpful.*

- *Thank you so much for requesting more details
  about [Product/Service]. Would you like to go ahead
  and make a booking/buy/place an order?*
- *I'm checking you received the info I sent over about
  (product/service)? Shall I get you booked in now for
  your first session? Or is there anything else we need
  to cover off first? Let me know, excited to start
  working with you!*
- *Hey Anna, I haven't heard back from you since I
  sent the proposal last week, and a couple of
  messages - I don't want to rush you, but I do want
  to make sure you received the info ok? Can you let
  me know? Chat soon, Anna*
- *Hey, I'm just checking in, did you want to go ahead
  with joining my membership/booking a package?*
- *Hi (name), I've sent you quite a few messages now
  and I haven't heard back from you at all, so I'm
  going to assume that you are no longer interested
  and I won't contact you about this again. I'd have
  loved to have supported you with (x). If you want to
  pick things up in the future then, please feel free to
  reach out, and I'd be delighted to help you. Best
  wishes, Anna*
- *How are you? It's been a while but I'm dropping you
  a line because although things didn't progress at
  the time, I know you were interested in X. I actually
  have an event next week designed to help people
  who want X so i instantly thought of you - please let
  me know if you'd like me to send you the details.*

Post-Purchase Follow-Up:

- *Thank you so much for joining my membership! I just wanted to say hi, thank you, and check in to see how you're getting on? We are here to help so please do reach out. Will I see you on the Q&A call next week?*
- *Thank you so much for your recent order! I hope you love your new outfit as much as I loved designing it! Please tag me on Instagram when you wear it so I can see those sparkles in real life, and if you wouldn't mind, I'd be so grateful if you could click here to leave us a review. Thanks so much again, as a small independent business, your custom means the world to me!*

After a Networking Event:

- *It was great meeting you at [Event]. I was really intrigued by what you said about [topic discussed]. Let's catch up over a call or a coffee soon to discuss. Are you available on [date/time]?*
- *It was great meeting you at [Event] today. As promised here is the link to my free online sales strategy scorecard where you can get a personalised report advising you on next steps. www.annapayne.online/quiz Once you have completed it I will look at your results and then drop you another message to discuss next steps based on those insights. All the best and chat soon.*

When It Is OK NOT to Sell (in fact, I actively advise it!)

Having a values based business means you have clearly defined values and whenever you face a difficult decision or are uncertain which way to go, you use your values as your north star and decision making framework.

Throughout this book the assumption is that anything you sell is in the customer's best interests, and that you sell products and services which are fit for purpose and your business and sales strategy align with your values.

My values (freedom, integrity, generosity, love and live more if you're interested!) guide my actions and decisions through all sorts of strategic and tactical decisions.

I spend a lot of my working life telling people how to make more sales. This whole book is about how to make more sales, *but* there are times when you should not sell. Short-term pain (maybe) for longer-term gain.

A lot of people struggle in their business either in actual client delivery, client complaints or missed payments and broken contracts. All a huge headache, distracting you from what you really want to do.

It often comes down to:

1. Taking on non-ideal clients, either through a sense of desperation (need all the sales you can get) or because you feel an obligation to serve anyone and everyone.

2. Selling offers that aren't good enough or you don't
   have capacity to deliver on.

For any of us who work closely with clients, taking on non-ideal clients or making sales against your better judgement from a sense of obligation or desperation can prove a huge time, energy and joy suck.

Let's assume you will always deliver with excellence and you are not obligated to sell to anyone you don't want to.

The time you save by cutting out clients who drain your time and energy can be used to work on converting even more clients.

For this reason, I regularly say no thank you to one-to-one work. Even more frequently I see people giving me buying signals which I don't follow up on because I know I don't want to work with that person. This may sound harsh but it's an integrity thing. Reasons can range from: I have no capacity, to I don't think their needs match my skill set and I'm not the best person for the job, through to less tangible, gut instincts about people I don't gel or connect with, people I'm not sure are ready/willing/able to do the work, and more fundamentally people I don't feel I'll enjoy working with! So I say no thank you. It's a good thing for me and for them.

When I first had to recruit and build my own team, the best advice I ever got was to hire on values, ethos and strengths. Ask yourself, would you like to go for dinner and drinks with this person? (Or would it be painfully awkward?)

I ask that question of myself when it comes to close contact client work. Life is too short to do work you don't love. More than that, if I know my heart will sink every time I see someone's name in my diary, I'd be doing them a complete injustice by taking their cash!

I will not accept your money if I don't:

A) Love your vision, believe in you, and feel excited about your business, AND

B) Believe that together we can achieve the results you are looking for.

Beyond that ever so important human connection and chemistry piece being right, I won't work with certain types of organisations that don't align with my values, for example, those that exploit or are harmful, that have anything to do with arms, or that test on animals.

That's being guided by my values and personal preferences, and protecting my integrity, my peace of mind, my reputation and my relationships. These are sacred. And although I can sell a lot of things, I will only sell what I wholeheartedly believe in. You should too.

Part 6

Deliver with Excellence

Vision: Define your goals and set targets for a clear, focused approach.

Audience: Get visible with a clear, compelling message to build your audience.

Lead Generation: Take daily action to generate and nurture leads.

Unlock sales: Make compelling offers and convert leads into sales.

Excellence: Deliver with excellence and leverage your success.

Chapter 18
Deliver With Excellence

Running a business is busy and entrepreneurs often have a lot of different plates spinning, along with a real urgency around generating revenue. It is understandable that quick wins are tempting. I love a quick, easy win as much as the next person.

Quick wins are good. But short-term results should never be at the expense of your longer-term success and in particular your focus on long-term relationships.

One of the worst things you can do is invest all your efforts into getting new clients, but drop the ball when it comes to delivery and retention because you are focusing too much attention on looking for new clients. You over-promise and under-deliver. (If you are a service business owner and you don't have time to properly service your clients, this is often a sign you are under-charging. Go back and make sure your price and profit margin are appropriate for the time, resources and effort required to deliver with excellence, and make the required adjustments.

If you drop the ball on delivery or service, life becomes harder because you might have complaints to deal with. Or refund requests. Even if you don't, you'll definitely have people out there saying non-complimentary things to their friends and peers if they haven't had a good experience.

So when you close a sale, don't see this as the end of the sales process. See it as just the beginning of a thriving business relationship that lasts the test of time. Treat it with respect and care.

This isn't only important from a quality and integrity perspective; it is good business sense. As we have talked about all the way through this book, integrity, quality, long-term thinking and client relationships are key to your success and yes, to the number of sales you make and to your earning potential.

Client relationships should always be about the long game, creating loyal clients who are with you for the long term and not only recommend you to others but buy from you time and time again. The way to do this is through delivering with excellence.

Delivering With Excellence Secures:

- Your reputation and integrity and feeling good about what you do
- Case studies, reviews and feedback that you can leverage for more sales

- Referrals
- Repeat purchases
- Upsells
- Customers who do your marketing for you because they talk so highly of what you do and mention your business to other prospective customers

---

Remember, when you deliver with excellence, you're not just closing a sale, it's not the end. It is the beginning of what has the potential to be a positive client relationship that adds value to your business for many years to come.

---

* * *

It Is Way Easier to Sell to Existing Clients than to New Clients

There is a wealth of research showing that it is significantly easier to sell to people who have already bought from you than it is to acquire new customers.

- The probability of selling to an existing customer is sixty to seventy percent while the probability of selling to a new prospect is five to twenty percent.
- Existing customers are fifty percent more likely to try new products and spend thirty-one percent more compared to new customers.

- Increasing customer retention rates by five percent can increase profits from twenty-five percent to ninety-five percent.
- It can cost five times more to attract a new customer than to retain an existing one.

These statistics show the value of customer retention and the importance of focusing on delivering excellence to existing customers to leverage additional sales opportunities.

* * *

Your Checklist to Delivering With Excellence

☐ Be clear on deliverables and terms of purchase

☐ Do what you say you will, when you say you will do it

☐ Keep clear, open communication

☐ Be honest if things don't go according to plan and find solutions

☐ See things from your client's perspective

☐ Review client satisfaction levels formally and informally to identify any points of friction and look for all opportunities to improve

☐ Commit to continual evolution

☐ Charge high enough prices that you can provide at the required standard

☐ Look for opportunities to elevate the client experience and surprise and delight them with small but thoughtful additional touches. The joy is in the extra.

To Maximise Your Potential in This Area:

1. Make sure you have follow on products and services and offer these to your existing clients.
2. Leverage great delivery by asking for testimonials and reviews to use in your marketing.
3. Ask them to refer others to you and consider whether you want to incentivise your referrals with a rewards scheme.

Part 7

What Next? Your Daily Tasks

It is good to know that you have it within your power to effect change and drive results, and you really do. Your actions will drive your results.

When it comes to sales success, it is all about doing the right things consistently. The more consistent you get, the better results you will see. Boring? Maybe. But when you see the results, then it becomes super exciting. You'll be far too busy delivering and celebrating your growth and success to feel bored.

Performing some regular tasks on a daily, weekly and monthly basis will help you. I've suggested some key tasks to focus on. The easiest way to make sure these tasks are done is to book the time into your calendar.

Daily Tasks

Visibility: Dedicate time each day to increasing visibility among new and existing audiences across various platforms.

Sales First Hour: Spend one hour exclusively on sales activities, including new lead generation, starting conversations and follow-ups.

Lead Engagement and Tracking: Actively engage with and track your leads daily, focusing on relationship nurturing and offering tailored solutions.

Start 10+ New Meaningful Conversations: Initiate over ten meaningful conversations daily with potential clients or partners on social media or other platforms.

Weekly Tasks

Message All New Social Media Connections: Send personal messages to all new social media connections to establish a rapport and open communication channels.

Weekly actions and goals: Set yourself non-negotiable tasks and goals to achieve that week.

Review: Assess your progress against your weekly goals, identifying areas of success and improvement.

Check-in with Lapsed Clients: Reach out to clients you haven't heard from in a while to rekindle the relationship and explore potential needs.

Upgrade Opportunities with Existing Clients: Check in with current clients to identify those who might be ready for an upgrade or additional services.

Networking and Partnership Development: Actively seek opportunities for networking and collaborations to create new opportunities and build your audience.

Reviews: Request reviews and feedback, and follow up on any reviews outstanding.

Monthly Tasks

Business Performance Review: Review your business's performance against monthly goals, review key metrics and performance of sales pages, funnels, etc.

Goal Setting: Set and refine goals for the upcoming month based on the month's outcomes.

Reflection: Reflect on your successes, celebrate wins, and look for the learning from challenges.

Client Experience Improvement: Find opportunities to enhance the overall experience for your existing clients.

Additional Suggestions for Sales-Driving Activities

- **Webinar Hosting or Participation**: Regularly host or participate in webinars to showcase your expertise and engage with a broader audience.

- **Offer Limited-Time Promotions**: Create urgency and attract new clients by offering limited-time promotions or discounts.
- **Customer Referral Programme**: Implement a referral programme that incentivises existing clients to refer new clients.
- **Strategic Email Marketing**: Use email marketing to keep in touch with your leads and clients, providing them with valuable content and updates.
- **Collaborate on Content Creation**: Collaborate with influencers or other businesses to create content that can reach new audiences.

Incorporating these activities into your routine can significantly enhance your sales efforts, ensuring a consistent approach to business growth and client engagement.

Mantras to Live by

There are two concepts/mantras that I have found transformative in my own business journey and which I share with clients over and over again. In fact, if you ever work in person with me, you'll see both written on a post-it note stuck to my laptop to serve as a reminder if I ever need it.

- Imperfect Authentic Action (#IAA)
- Do One Thing Today (#DOTT)

Imperfect Authentic Action: Do that thing. Go before you feel fully ready. Because you never feel fully ready until you start and do the thing, so pushing yourself out of your comfort zone with courage is the only way to build the confidence to feel ready.

Do One Thing Today: Make sure that every single day, no matter how small it is, you take a step towards your big goals... not just treading water but moving forward.

I have trained myself over a period of years to put these into action, and you can too. The idea is to take frequent imperfect or messy action and make consistent moves forward, no matter how small. Even when things aren't perfect, imperfect action will always trump perfect inaction.

This isn't about shoddy work or poor quality; it is about making things the best you can at the time, with the resources you have and just getting things done. The approach encourages people to embrace progress over perfection, to learn from their mistakes, and to keep moving forward towards their goals. No more waiting until you have just one more qualification, until you have got your website done, agonising over fonts and colours, or waiting until some future point when all the stars align and you feel ready. Really you just need to get your offer out there and talk about it with the right people.

Have the courage to commit to imperfect action and the consistency to do this daily.

There's a common misconception that success requires massive, dramatic actions. It is the small, consistent steps that build momentum and lead to sustainable progress.

Each day, by doing just one thing related to your goals, you stack up victories, learning, and you move forward.

If every day, no matter how small, you take one step towards your goals, within three months you'll be much further ahead. This is way more productive than waiting until you have the right time and conditions to make a big leap (because when will the conditions ever be right?).

Do one thing today, or #DOTT, came about when I was trying to build a business with a baby and a toddler and it was very hard some days. I didn't want to tread water and work hard just to stay still so I had a rule that in addition to the daily operational tasks, I had to do one extra thing every day that was going to move the business forward. Even if it was one ten-minute job in the evening, I did one thing around sales/business growth. Maybe it was a lead generation post, a follow-up phone call, a message about a collaboration, or an email to my list. Do one thing today (and every day) that is not just a run-of-the-mill job, but something extra which moves you towards your goals.

We hold back because of fear. Fear of failure, fear of looking silly, fear of what people might think of us...

We do it all the time. I sometimes catch myself doing it too... We don't want to acknowledge that it is fear so we tell ourselves stories about waiting for the right time, waiting until we have more time, waiting until the kids are older, waiting until we've sorted our website, waiting until we've completed a qualification, waiting until we lose weight, waiting until the stars align and the conditions are perfect. I have been personally guilty of all of the above. These days I am just better at calling myself out on my own excuses.

There is always a reason to wait. There is never a right time. There is only time and what you choose to do with it. So, where are you waiting? And why? What one action can you take today, right now, to take yourself one step closer to your goals?

Do not spend forever waiting for the right time to take the perfect giant leap. Take small, often messy or imperfect, steps consistently.

I believe you already know the one thing you really could and should do today to take a step toward your goals. Stop waiting and start moving. Take the steps forward in your business.

Your Takeaway: Have the courage to make a move. Work with the resources you have *now*.

Chapter 19

Shall We Work Together on Your Sales?

I would truly love to support you in the next steps of your sales success and business growth.

First of all, let's connect online. Come and find me on Instagram, Facebook or LinkedIn. I would love you to tell me that you've read this book so tag me in your stories and posts, and send me a message to let me know your biggest takeaways and what action you're going to take.

Visit www.annapayne.online/book to discover all the free resources, tools and templates that are referred to in the book. Download them and implement the strategies.

If you'd like to learn more about working together on your sales and success, I'd be over the moon! Come to www.annapayne.online and go to the 'everything' page www.annapayne.online/everything, where you'll always see an up to date and comprehensive list of every single free and paid offer and way to work with me.

My low-cost monthly membership is the most wonderful community of business owners, there to support each other, collaborate and take consistent action with their sales.

You can also access courses and training, and work with me more closely if you'd like that support. You can drop me an email at anna@annapayne.online or a direct message on Instagram. I'd love to hear from you and chat about the next steps.

Glossary

Here are some commonly used terms in sales and marketing:

1. **A/B Testing:** A method where two versions of an ad, webpage, or other content are compared to determine which performs better in terms of engaging users or driving conversions.
2. **Acquisition:** The process of acquiring new customers or clients for your business.
3. **Affiliate Marketing:** A type of performance-based marketing where businesses reward external partners (affiliates) for generating traffic or sales through the affiliate's marketing efforts.
4. **B2B (Business-to-Business):** Companies that sell products or services directly to other businesses.
5. **B2C (Business-to-Consumer):** Companies that sell products or services directly to individual consumers.
6. **Branding:** The process of creating a unique image and name for a product or business in the consumers' minds.
7. **Churn Rate:** The percentage of subscribers or users who stop using a product or service during a specific time frame.
8. **Conversion:** The act of a potential customer taking the desired action, such as making a purchase, signing up for a newsletter, or filling out a contact form.
9. **CRM (Customer Relationship Management):** A system or platform used to manage a company's interactions with its customers or potential customers.
10. **CTA (Call to Action):** A prompt that encourages the audience to take a specific action, like 'Buy Now' or 'Learn More'.
11. **Demographics:** Specific characteristics such as age, gender, income, and education.
12. **Funnel:** A model that represents the stages of a buyer's journey, from the first interaction to the final sale. (Also Sales Funnel or Customer Journey.)
13. **Inbound Marketing:** Marketing strategies that focus on attracting customers through relevant and helpful content, rather than pushing

products or services onto prospects. Also referred to as Attraction Marketing.

14. **KPI (Key Performance Indicator):** A measurable value which demonstrates how effectively a company is achieving its key business objectives.

15. **Lead:** An individual or organisation that expresses interest in a product or service.

16. **Margin:** The difference between the sales price of a product and the cost of producing it.

17. **Outbound Marketing:** Traditional forms of marketing, such as TV ads, radio ads, print ads and cold calls, whereby companies push their message out.

18. **Prospect:** A potential customer who fits the target market but hasn't yet expressed interest.

19. **ROI (Return on Investment):** A measurement of the profitability of an investment. It is calculated as the net profit from the investment divided by the cost of the investment.

20. **Segmentation:** The process of dividing a market into distinct subsets of consumers with common needs or characteristics.

21. **SEO (Search Engine Optimisation):** The process of improving a website or online content to increase its visibility in search engine results.

22. **Target Market:** A specific group of potential buyers for whom a business positions its products and services. Also known as Ideal Client.

23. **USP (Unique Selling Proposition):** A factor that differentiates a product from its competitors, such as the highest quality, the lowest cost, or the first-ever product of its kind.

24. **Value Proposition:** A clear statement that explains how a product solves a customer's problem, delivers specific benefits, and tells the ideal customer why they should buy from this company and not from the competition.

25. **Webinar:** A training or presentation delivered over the internet, sometimes live, sometimes pre-recorded.

Acknowledgements

This feels a bit like an Oscars acceptance speech, but there are so many people I'd like to acknowledge for their help and support and for their belief in me. They have made this book possible. So here goes, in the full knowledge that if this was an Oscars speech they'd be playing the music halfway through.

Thank you to the team at Authors & Co for helping me get this book out of my head and into the world, for encouraging me and believing in the book before I'd written a single word, and for being endlessly patient and trusting even as the deadline was fast approaching.

To Dani Wallace who helped me clarify my message for speaking on stage, which has helped so much in the creation of this book.

To Lisa Johnson for trusting me with your audience as your Associate Sales Coach, and for the opportunities to work with Authors & Co and Dani.

Thank you to all the good role models, mentors and leaders I have had the pleasure to work with and know over the years. It makes sense to surround yourself with smart people and I'm so grateful to each of you for what you've seen in me and helped me to see in myself.

And thank you to some of those salespeople who have tried to make me feel like I am less than enough, to get me to buy from them. Thank you for inspiring me to do things differently and to get that message out there to more people and create a positive ripple of change in the world of entre-preneurship.

To Ashley, Sam, Yvonne and Lynsey, my team who support me daily in so many ways, and not only make business feel easier but way more fun too. I'd be lost without you. You have gone way beyond being people I work with and are my forever friends. Love you all.

To my friend and coach, Emma. I wrote this book as a sprint rather than a marathon because that's how my brain works, but I've also looked after myself throughout the process! Emma has reminded me to eat well, to sleep well, to drink three litres of water a day, do my daily steps and sometimes even work out while writing this book! My stress response is usually to put myself last on the list of things that need to be looked after, but you are helping me learn new and better habits and I feel healthier and happier since working with you.

Huge and most grateful thanks to all my clients who do the work, who show up, who have big dreams about the changes they want to make, the goals they want to achieve and who amaze me, inspire me and make my job never feel like work. To those inside my membership. To Gemma, who was on my first ever group programme in 2020 and was the first person to join my membership when it opened and is now a great friend. I attract the best people and so many of my clients have so often gone on to become friends and collaborators. I'm so grateful and send so much love to you all.

Thank you to all my family. My biggest support and my happiest place.

To Ava and Lewis, my proudest achievement is being your Mum. You two are loved beyond belief and you've inspired me more than you'll ever know. Being Mum is the greatest job I will ever do, and we have so many more adventures to look forward to. As a lot of these adventures involve going to faraway places, I always have a meaningful driver to help me earn money. I love you both with no end, the moon, the stars and the waves. It is no coincidence that I have been most focused and most successful since you two came along.

To Keith, my husband, for his belief in me, his love and encouragement, his ideas and his wise advice. For supporting my ideas, some crazy, some less so, for helping me know which risks are worth taking, and for supporting every step I take even when the end result isn't clear. Thank you too for the practical support, not least the slack at home while I have been writing this book, the lifts to the airport, and all the hundreds of ways you make my life easier. It's all those little threads. I love this life we are building together for our family and I am so grateful to have your support.

To my Mum and Dad for bringing me up to believe that I was loved, that I was smart, that I could do anything I set my mind to and that I had the right to be seen, be heard and have opinions. Society tries to knock that out of you over the years, especially as a woman, so I am forever grateful for their love and belief in me that is programmed in and always there inside me when I need it.

And to my Mum for being the person who told me to set up my first group coaching programme straight away and go for it now, when I told her it was my future goal and gave her some waffle about waiting for the right time. And who was my first reader of this book and as always gave me nothing but love and support.

To my sister Chloe, my biggest cheerleader, best friend, neighbour and the person who just gets me and is always there to look after me, love me, have a kitchen disco and make me laugh until I cry, just when I need it most. Life is busy but I hope you know how much I love and appreciate you.

And finally, thank you to you for picking up this book, for getting this far and for the inspiration of knowing that people will read this book, take action and create results.

I wish you nothing but success and happiness, and for your business to unlock and support everything that you want in life and more.

Together, let's create more amazing businesses and positive change in the world.

Anna x